CHAD ALLEN

RISE UP, DAD!

How to Embrace Your Role as the Spiritual Leader of
Your Family in a World Gone Mad

First edition

ISBN (paperback): 979-8-9916174-2-0
ISBN (hardcover): 979-8-9916174-3-7

This book was professionally typeset on Reedsy.
Find out more at reedsy.com

This book is dedicated to all men, husbands, and fathers who want to positively impact their children, wives, and nation. God has entrusted you to help save the family and nation from destruction.

Contents

Acknowledgments

To my amazingly beautiful wife, your testament of faith and encouragement is nothing short of amazing. You truly excel in all areas and are a stunning example to me as your husband and to our children. You exemplify what it means to be a Proverbs 31 woman.

To my incredible children, you are a blessing from above. I am excited to see how God uses you to impact the lives of millions. You are truly blessed!

To those who supported me, I am honored and grateful that you have prayed for me, blessed me, and encouraged me when things seemed impossible. Your examples are to be followed in how to be courageous and confident in times of blessing and difficulty.

I want to give a special shout out to my Filipino family and friends, who helped me through the difficult and joyous times when I lived in the Philippines. Your support helped change my perspective on my faith journey, and you helped mold me into the kind of man, husband, and father I am today.

I want to thank Job Eloja for helping me put together this book. Your devotion and help are amazing. Thank you for being there!

To Pastor Dr. Dave Magalong, your lessons on biblical manhood made me realize the importance of it as a husband and father. Your knowledge on the subject is amazing. You are like a father in how you teach. Thank you!

Introduction

Rise Up, Dad! If you haven't noticed, you are fighting an uphill battle against forces unseen and a society that desires to make you less impactful as a father within the family.

As a dad, God created you to exhibit certain characteristics that empower you to excel in your role as a man, husband, and father. It is innate in you, regardless of how the world tries to remove those characteristics from you.

The war on dads is not a recent phenomenon; in fact, it has been a war since creation itself. Why? Because you hold the key that holds your family together, a protective barrier against the world and principalities that want you out of the picture and your children influenced by sources other than you.

Recently, fathers began to be attacked and made weak, most notably during the sexual revolution of the 60s. We then saw the destruction of the black family, followed by the white and Asian communities. At the same time, we began to see the killing of babies through abortion. This, in turn, has now created a warped culture that has normalized violence, gender confusion, the killing of babies, depression, and the weakening of the father and family.

As a father, you protect your family against these things. You are the spiritual leader of your family, the protector—the band that holds your marriage and children together. You are vital to ensuring that a nation turning dark returns to the light of Christ.

In my previous Dad Creed Book - The Dad Creed: Understanding the Role of Fatherhood for a Meaningful Impact, I shared what has worked for me as a dad. While that book was a quick overview, many were hoping that the book was longer. This book adds to what is discussed in the first Dad Creed book by diving deeper into the dad's role. Further, others stated that they wish it didn't have a Christian overtone. I want to state that I understand where you are coming from; however, when it comes to this particular topic and how it is presented, it is hard to present this topic without incorporating Christian and Jewish principles.

In this book, I encourage you to stand in the gap for your family by understanding your role as a father. This spiritual father's head protects his family against the elements of an evil culture striving to destroy the very fabric of what is good in Christ. This book will help you understand the importance of blessing your children daily with spiritual protection and preparing them for adulthood, where they may have to stand firm for the truth.

It is time for dads around America and the world to regain control of their families, move their families forward in Christ, and heal their families and nations.

I

RISE UP, DAD!

How to Embrace Your Role as the Spiritual Leader of Your Family in a World Gone Mad

Chapter 1: What's the Deal with a Dad Movement?

Back in grade school, our Social Studies would tell us that the family is the basic unit of society. With that, family is essentially the foundation of our nation. The United States of America as we know it would not exist if not for the millions of families that live in it. And our family values are one thing that makes this country great.

Unfortunately, the family is no longer the same. Many modern families are fragmented. The sense of unity in the family has been lost. The worst part is it's the children who are suffering the most.

We see fatherless kids, abandoned kids, kids who long for the love of a dad. Statistics from 2022 show that about 18.3 million American children live without a father at home. Growing up fatherless has a profound negative impact on children.

Not only that. There's also the other side of the coin – children who did grow up with fathers, but their dads were abusive, neglectful, or detached.

Maybe these fathers think that their only role in the family is to work and earn money. As long as they bring home the bacon, they can do anything they want. They spend inordinate amounts of time – and money – on hobbies, peers, and themselves. Nothing wrong with any of these, but when it costs them their families, it becomes a bad thing.

Some fathers would indulge themselves in alcohol or drugs and get addicted. Their addictions then control their lives – their decisions always revolve around drinking more or using more. Consequently, they become abusive to their families. Their wives and children bear the brunt of their substance abuse. They unfortunately become victims of verbal abuse, assault, and neglect. Some mothers would even resort to abandoning their abusive husbands for the sake of their and their own children's well-being. They would rather raise their kids in a fatherless home than an abusive home. And you can't blame them; they are only doing what is best for their families given their situations. Dire circumstances can force people to make drastic, difficult decisions.

Other fathers would resort to becoming workaholics – their jobs become their "drugs." They get addicted to working, and their families pay the price. Because these fathers are mostly away for work, their wives and kids get very little time with them. That miniscule amount of time is barely enough to build a good relationship with their families. For sure, their wives and children clamor for more time with them. Love is best spelled as T-I-M-E, after all.

Even fathers who spend a good deal of time at home can still be neglectful. David Walsh, founder of Mind Positive Parenting, found that school-aged boys only spend around 30 minutes *per week* talking to their dads one-on-one. That's all the mentoring and serious talk they get with their dads.

Certainly, children need a lot more attention from their fathers than just 30 minutes a week. So how do they fill that need for attention? The Internet. Online gaming, YouTube, TikTok, Netflix, you name it. If these kids can't get it from their fathers, they get it from the Internet. Data from 2020 show that school-age boys clock in more than 40 hours per week watching TV, gaming, and Internet browsing. That's as much as working a full-time job. With these numbers, it's as if these boys hold full-time jobs entertaining themselves!

A clear consequence of this is children are getting their values from the Internet instead of their fathers. As a dad, it is your responsibility to impart Godly character to your children. But if you barely have time for them, you cannot fulfill this responsibility.

Actually, the decline of fatherhood is not so much a recent event. This had started in the 1960s during the so-called "sexual revolution." At that time, feminism also became popular, and so did the belief that women and men can have sex with anyone they want at any time. The idea of waiting to get married was questioned and devalued. More people, especially young ones at the time, wanted to explore their sexualities unhinged.

As a consequence of this sexual revolution, men were less expected to be heads of the household. Also, the ideals of feminism influenced more women to further their careers and earn more. These ideals even empowered some women to take on leadership roles previously dominated by men.

Not that the idea of female empowerment is a bad thing in itself. What's concerning is its unintended consequences on men and fatherhood. In modern families, it's not unusual to observe the women being the actual head of the household. Men, on the other hand, are more passive and uninvolved with family life.

This creates a crisis for dads everywhere in America. More fathers are either completely absent or present but passive. They spend miniscule amounts of time with their wives and children. They are no longer serving as the mentors they ought to be for their kids. And they no longer serve as the leaders of the home. Instead, they become content being passive, letting their families' lives slip past them. They don't care enough to be involved in their children's lives.

Overall, our culture has created entire generations of fatherless children. Though the failed fathering was not their fault, they are now reaping the consequences.

Effects of fatherless homes on children

Children who grew up in fatherless homes face a myriad of challenges later in life. For one, they do not have a role model for manhood. Their mothers may have taught them principles of masculinity, but that's not enough. They need an actual example to follow – a father figure. If they don't have that, knowing how to become a man becomes a huge challenge.

Mental health problems are also rampant in fatherless kids. Several studies have shown that fatherless children are vulnerable to low self-worth, attachment issues, aggression, anxiety, depression, social withdrawal, and suicidal tendencies.

The effects on children's sense of self-worth are the most damaging. Without fathers to affirm their value, these kids would feel inferior to their peers who have fathers. Also, it is common for kids to blame themselves for why their fathers are not present, even if it isn't their fault.

This kind of thinking may be reinforced when these children enter school. They see their classmates with complete families or hear their stories about their dads. Pretty soon, the kids from fatherless homes will ask questions. They will wonder why their dads are not with them. They will wonder why they live with only one parent. They will envy the other kids who have loving fathers. Then, at some point, they will think they have done something that contributed to their being fatherless. It's an unhealthy mindset, and it will mess them up early in life.

Aggression issues are also common for children who grew up in fatherless homes, particularly in the teenage and adolescent years. One of the father's roles is to teach kids how to control themselves. Without that, children have no strong authority figure to look up to. They have no one to show them how to handle their anger and any intense negative emotions. Because of this, they tend to become aggressive as they grow older.

Problems with authority also stem from the lack of a father figure. Ideally, a child growing up with a father at home sees him as a figure of discipline. The child wants to behave properly and follow the rules, otherwise his dad will scold him. Of course, the child does not want punishment or negative consequences, so he tends to follow the rules. This dynamic at home is one way children learn to give respect to authority figures. Without the father to model discipline, children tend to grow up defiant.

Aside from these, fatherless homes lead to kids who perform poorly in school and later in life. Fatherless children are more likely to drop out of school and make decisions that are not good for their future. Some would join gangs and get involved in crime. Some would take substances and get addicted to them. Without fathers to guide them in making the right choices, they are prone to making bad decisions that will destroy their lives.

The forgotten roles of the father

Many fathers today see themselves as just providers of their families – and nothing else. They would think that as long as their families eat three meals a day, have a roof over their heads, and they can pay all their bills on time, it's all good. They have fulfilled the role of a father.

Here's another thing. Fulfilling the role of provider is a tough job. Some dads work jobs they don't even like just to bring food to the table. Some even have to work more than one job to make ends meet. In turn, they have very little time to spend with their families. So I can't really blame the dads who have to work so hard and spend most of their time earning a living. I totally understand how hard that must be.

Even then, being a father is not just about provision. Sure, it's one of the primary roles of a father; we cannot discount that. No good dad wants his family to starve or go homeless, after all. Thing is, provision is only one of the important roles of a dad to his family. Fathers also need to be three things:

1. Leader of the home
2. Lover of his wife
3. Mentor of his children

Most dads often neglect these roles. They are equally important, as the father must act as the "director" of his family. Take a look at the role of a director in movies. He's the one who guides the actors and crew to achieve the scenes he wants for the movie. In the same way, the dad is the one who guides his wife and kids in the direction he envisions for his family. And he doesn't just tell them what to do; he leads by his example. He shows his family what he wants to happen and the steps they need to take to achieve it.

Also, in the film industry, a director does not act on his own. He is accountable to the producer, who gives the director the resources he needs to create the film. If the director creates the film the way the producer wants it, the producer is happy. He may give additional budget to the director, or he may give him incentives for a job well done.

In the same way, a father is accountable to a Producer – the Heavenly Father – for the way he directs his family. This is where leadership comes in. If he leads his family in a way that pleases the Heavenly Father, the Heavenly Father is pleased and blesses the dad. Those blessings are like incentives – they can be financial bonuses or immaterial forms of wealth. A good relationship with his wife and children, for one, is a great blessing for the dad. A peaceful home is another. We often take these immaterial blessings for granted, but they definitely make life a lot better!

A particularly important role of the dad is to mentor his children. There is an old proverb that goes, "Train up a child in the way he should go, and when he is old he will not depart from it." If you have a Bible at home or on your phone, you can find that line in Proverbs 22:6. With that, you as a father ought to be your children's trainer. You need to teach them how to be righteous persons who please their Heavenly Father. And if you teach them these ways, according to the proverb, they will not forget these principles even when they grow older. When they become adults, they will still behave the way you taught them to when they were little. Most importantly, they will make good decisions on their own. They will be able to make choices that will benefit their lives because they know right from wrong. This way, they will live in ways that honor both you, their earthly father, and their Heavenly Father.

Aside from these, let's not forget a critical role of the father – as a lover of his wife. Many dads often neglect this role. As a consequence, many mothers do not feel loved at home. They feel inadequate and undervalued. Some feel like they are just servants at home instead of wives. It is the duty of the husband to make sure his wife feels loved, secured, and treasured. This is especially important because your kids are watching. How you treat their mom will stick to their minds until they grow up. For your sons, in particular, this will be their model in how they will treat their future wives. For your daughters, this is how they will perceive men when they become adults.

These important roles of a father are often overlooked in our culture. Most people are obsessed with acquiring wealth, thinking it's the best way to give their families a good life. They want to buy big houses, drive nice cars, and take vacations all around the world. All the more because they see everyone else doing those things on social media. But again, providing for the family is just one thing a father must do. And society's idea of a "good life" still leaves a lot to be desired.

Why a Dad Movement?

As dads, it is up to us to protect our families from the ills of society around us. This is especially true for our kids, who ultimately pay the price for fathers neglecting their important roles. But none of us can do it on our own.

The hope of this Dad Movement is to create a community of like-minded fathers. Our goal is to win back our families from the culture around us that seeks to destroy the family. With this community, none of us will think we are alone in this journey of fatherhood.

We can support each other, learn from each other, and encourage each other when the going gets tough. Our families are counting on us to lead them. We will need all the help we can get to direct our families towards the right path.

Most importantly, a community of dads will allow us to pray for each other. Our Heavenly Father is with us in this journey, and He is always willing to help us out. If we ask Him to show us how to be good fathers, He will give us wisdom. We can definitely help each other, too, through prayer and sharing our experiences.

Join the Facebook group, a community of dads supporting each other
https://www.facebook.com/groups/816737610648654

Chapter 2: Every Dad is a Soldier

Being a dad is much like being a soldier. You may not think of it that way, especially because you don't actually hold rifles, fire cannons, or dodge enemy bullets. If you happen to be in the service, you may also not think of fatherhood to be something like a battlefield. After all, home life is generally peaceful compared to the battlefield. Thing is, it's a different kind of battle when it comes to your family.

In the home, everything may be safe and peaceful, but out there it's a battlefield. That conflict is not fought with bombs or bullets, but with words and ideas. The postmodern culture is at war with the Godly culture we want our children to imbibe. Postmodern culture is flinging arrows at your children left and right. It's easy for them to get hit. When they do, they'd be influenced by the wrong ideas.

Postmodernism has one key principle I absolutely disagree with. It's the idea that there is no such thing as absolute truth. In other words, all truth is relative. It depends on what you feel about it. If you feel good about something, then that is your truth. If others don't feel good about that same thing, it's not their truth. With postmodernism, anyone can define truth. There is no reliable frame of reference.

Think of this example. I believe that stealing is wrong, no matter what your circumstances in life. Now, suppose my friend believes stealing is okay in certain situations. For instance, if he's struggling to put food on the table for his family, it becomes okay to shoplift. For him, the concept of "stealing is always wrong" is not true. He has a different truth: "Stealing is okay when you're financially struggling."

In postmodernist thought, both versions are acceptable. "Stealing is wrong" is true, and "stealing is not always wrong" is also true. My version of truth and my friend's version of truth both have merit. Thing here is, both versions contradict each other. Stealing cannot be wrong and right at the same time. It has to be either one.

In the field of philosophy and logic, there's a principle called the Law of Non-Contradiction. Simply stated, two opposing versions of something cannot both be true at the same time. So, stealing cannot both be wrong and not wrong. It has to be one or the other.

But who's to say stealing is wrong or not? Who has the higher authority in determining truth – me or my friend? We are both human beings, and honestly, no one can say that one of us is higher than the other.

But if there is a higher standard we can refer to, then it's easier to find out what the truth is. Let's refer to the Ten Commandments, which was a set of divine rules sent by the Heavenly Father to His people here on Earth, through their leader Moses. Commandment number 8 clearly says, "You shall not steal." (Exodus 20:15)

Since this command was given by God, we can say that it indeed came from a higher authority than humanity. That's why "stealing is wrong" is absolutely true on all fronts. It has become a moral principle that nearly all people live by, whether they believe in God or not.

Another postmodern invention is the idea that you can be any gender you want. The default male or female has become an "assigned sex at birth." It is no longer permanent, and it isn't defining. You can change it if you wish to. What's more baffling is that the change is not permanent, either. You can change your gender again at any time, so long as you feel you are of a different gender. Some people even declare themselves as "gender-fluid." That means, like a liquid, their gender flows from one form to another. The switch can happen at any time they choose, as long as they feel being a different gender at that moment. In other words, I can be male today, female tomorrow, and male again the day after.

These days, having a confused gender type is not just celebrated — it's encouraged. We see things like puberty blockers being pushed onto young children so they can be their preferred gender. Postmodern culture is actually telling our kids to mess with their natural biological functions. It would seem the culture does not want our kids to develop normally.

It's interesting to note that gender confusion used to be classified as a mental illness — it was called "gender identity disorder." Then, in 2013, it was not classified as a disorder. It is now called "gender dysphoria," and the change was made arguably to remove stigma around the condition.

Despite the reclassification, I still think there's something wrong with it. I hold firmly to the fact that we are born into this world either male or female. There is nothing in between or beyond those two. The Holy Scriptures mention in Genesis 1 that God created only male and female. If you are born male but desperately want to be female, then I'm sorry to say there is something wrong and you need help. Same goes with one born female who would move mountains to become male.

Another cultural phenomenon tearing our families apart comes through social media. This affects our kids primarily, as their minds are highly impressionable. They are the ones most vulnerable to popular influences. More so that our kids today get most of their knowledge from social media. Never mind if the information is right or wrong, as long as the number of likes, shares, and comments are high enough.

What I'm talking about are these mindless – and often harmful – TikTok challenges. There is one that encouraged young viewers to overdose on Benadryl, an allergy medicine. Kids who don't know any better take on the challenge, often to their detriment. You can clearly see its ill effects: In April of 2023, a 13-year-old boy from Ohio died of a Benadryl overdose as he attempted the senseless challenge.

Another is the so-called "Kia challenge" that sparked a spate of car thefts across Milwaukee in 2021. This trend continued and spread into Chicago in 2022. The perpetrators were often teenage boys, who were dubbed by the news media as the "Kia boys." The Kia challenge is even more atrocious because you can see the boys filming their crimes – from breaking into the cars to speeding with their heads hanging out of the windows. Many of those cars were even recklessly crashed and totaled.

These teens likely have an idea that stealing is wrong. But do they even know the consequences of their actions? Whether or not they do, the damage has been done. Hundreds of people lost their property. They have caused undue chaos and fear in the communities they live in. All this because they wanted to chase views, likes, and shares in the name of popularity. They won't even get rich doing such things.

This is the kind of culture we live in. It's what our kids have to contend with every single day. And if you give your kids free reign over their use of technology, you may not know what they're getting into. You may be in for a surprise when one day your child suddenly ends up in a police station or a hospital emergency room.

These bad influences in society are exactly why dads need to exercise leadership and authority in their families. You need to be the one to mentor your children to take the righteous path. Teach them how to make good decisions. Mold them to be individuals of noble character. Most importantly, lead your wife and treat her well, so your children will also follow your example when they decide to get married in the future.

Standing in the gap for your family

Standing in the gap means shielding your family from the arrows of postmodernism. You'll get hit instead of your family, but you don't want to take damage. For that, you need armor – the Scriptures call it the full armor of God. You can find the components of this armor in Ephesians 6:14-17:

- Belt of truth
- Breastplate of righteousness
- Shoes of the gospel of peace
- Shield of faith
- Helmet of salvation
- Sword of the spirit

The first five will protect you against the onslaught of the cruel world.

You also get an offensive weapon – the Sword of the spirit – for your counterattacks. Postmodernism flings falsehoods at your children, so the best thing to fight against these is the truth. Where can you get the truth? Go to the best Source – the Holy Scriptures.

I believe that the Bible is filled with lots of truths that form the foundation of a good life. As you learn from it, your children can learn from it as well. Pass the wisdom you gain onto them. Let them read the Word of God as well. With that, they will likewise be armed with the Sword of the spirit and be protected with the full armor of God. They, too, will be able to ward off the attacks of false ideologies and lies the world loves to throw at them.

To achieve these, you will need to exercise your leadership over your family. Ready to take on the challenge? The next chapter will show you how important it is to be the leader of your family and how you can rise up to fulfill the role.

Chapter 3: You are the Spiritual Head of Your Home

As fathers, we are meant to be the leaders of our families. Common knowledge would say that fathers are the head of the home, which means they are the ones who must take the lead. Think of the President of the United States. He leads the 50 states that are part of this country and guides them with principles of government. Without the leadership of the President, the USA would not be united. In the same way, the father is like the president of the family. He leads and governs all of his family's members.

Even the Holy Scriptures tell us a similar principle. Consider the story of Adam and Eve in the Garden of Eden. In the book of Genesis, Adam and Eve represented the first family on Earth. The first husband and wife, and the first father and mother to be. Of course, they did not have children yet at first. Theirs is a story of failed leadership, which then led to the Fall of Man. This is when all humanity became sinful, perpetrated by the actions of the first husband and wife.

Just to refresh your memory, here's how the story goes. We can find the story in Genesis 3 (please refer to a Bible for the full story). After God created everything on Earth, he created Adam and Eve, the first people. He put them in the Garden of Eden, where they can eat the fruit of any tree they wanted, except for one. That was the Tree of Knowledge of Good and Evil. That was the only tree God told them not to eat fruit from.

Then, a serpent tempted Eve, encouraging her to eat the fruit of the forbidden tree. Eve knew that God did not permit them to eat the fruit of that tree. But the serpent was persistent. He told Eve that when she eats the fruit, she will be like God, knowing good from evil.

At that point, Eve got excited at the prospect of being Godlike! That idea convinced her to take the forbidden fruit and eat it. He even gave some to Adam, and he ate it himself. Take note, both of them knew what God said about that tree and its fruit. God specifically gave them instructions not to eat the fruit of that tree. But Adam and Eve still chose to violate that rule.

What happened next? Adam and Eve saw that they were naked, and they felt ashamed. So they took some fig leaves and covered themselves. After that, they heard God walking in the garden, so they hid in the trees. Then God came looking for them. He called out to the man and asked where they were.

The man then said that he heard God in the garden, but he was afraid because he was naked, so he hid. God then asked him how he knew he was naked. That came with a follow-up question: Did you eat the fruit of the tree I told you not to? Adam then proceeded to blame Eve for giving him some of the fruit. God asked Eve what she had done, and Eve blamed the serpent for deceiving her.

That was the first sin. With that came the curse of mankind – all human beings that came after Adam and Eve would be born into a sinful world. The root cause? You could say it was because Adam and Eve did not follow God's command. That's absolutely right.

But we can see this story from another perspective. The story of the Fall of Man is a story of a failure of leadership.

God calls the man to be the leader of his family

Men being the leaders of their family is an implied role. God did not specifically tell Adam to "go and lead your family," but He called out to Adam first when he and Eve ate the forbidden fruit. But it was Eve who the serpent deceived, so why didn't God talk to Eve first?

The implication here is that God ordained Adam as the leader of his family. Though they did not have children yet, we can consider Adam and Eve as the first family. They were the first husband and wife couple, and that already counts as a family.

To understand this idea of male leadership further, let's consider the order of creation. In the second chapter of the book of Genesis, we can see that God created Adam first before Eve. He put Adam in the Garden of Eden to take care of it. Then God saw that Adam was alone, and he thought this wasn't good. So, God created Eve to be Adam's suitable companion.

Following that order, when the man and woman sinned, God called out to the man first. Why? Consider this perspective.

Suppose the serpent deceived Eve, as the story goes, but Adam talked Eve out of eating the forbidden fruit. Adam could have insisted on following God's orders. After all, God clearly told them not to eat fruit from the Tree of Knowledge of Good and Evil. But Adam didn't. Instead, he himself ate the forbidden fruit.

That is where it became a failure of leadership. Adam failed to lead Eve in doing the right thing. He even did the wrong thing himself, leading both of them into a crime. They both became violators of God's law, and the penalty was severe. Not only were they banned from the Garden of Eden permanently, but all of mankind were to suffer the consequences.

For Adam, his punishment was hard work to get food. Before, in the garden, all he had to do was pick any fruit when he was hungry – except for the fruit from the Tree of Knowledge of Good and Evil. Surely there were lots of other trees in the garden, so Adam and Eve had many choices. But because they violated God's command, Adam was cursed to toil before he could eat. By extension, all men who came after also had to work hard to earn a living and meet their basic needs.

For Eve, the punishment was twofold – pain in childbirth and the desire to control her husband. But God also said that the husband would rule over her. That leads to frustration. No wonder wives can become so angry with their husbands. It's bound to happen from the very beginning!

Going back to the area of Adam's leadership, we can see the consequences of his failure. Who gets to suffer those consequences? Everyone else. Everyone who would still be born in the future. One crucial failure affected the lives of untold millions.

Dads have become passive

We saw from the story in Genesis 3 that Adam did not exercise his leadership towards Eve. He very well knew what God commanded – to not eat the fruit of the Tree of Knowledge of Good and Evil. Yet when

Eve offered him that exact fruit, he caved in. He ate it, too. He could have told his wife off, that they need to follow what God commanded. But he didn't. He did not even say a word. Here's what we can read in Genesis 3:6: "She also gave some to her husband, who was with her, and he ate it." Adam just straight up ate it. We could even speculate that he didn't even stop to think if what he was about to do was right.

That's called being passive. Adam just let things pass, so both him and Eve ended up committing a huge sin against God. Had Adam exercised his leadership as the husband, he and Eve would have done the right thing.

How passivity is damaging your family

How about you as a husband and father? Have you also been acting passively? You may not notice it, but you can be a passive dad in many ways. The most striking example is in how much time you spend with your family. Answer these questions honestly:

1. When was the last time you went on a date with your wife? (That means just the two of you)
2. When was the last time you did something fun with your kids?
3. When was the last time you had a meal together with your whole family?
4. When was the last time you had a serious, focused conversation with your wife? With each of your children?

If your answers are either "a long time ago" or "I can't remember," that means you're spending too little time with your family. They long for your presence and attention! But they don't get those because either you're not there, or you're there but your mind is elsewhere. It's very possible to be at the same dinner table with your family while being mentally disconnected from them. If you're at dinner and everyone is on his or her phone, this is exactly what I mean. Everyone is tuned out. Their minds are somewhere else. The emotional connection is nowhere to be found. There's only food on the table, but not quality time.

Remember what I said in the first chapter – that love is best spelled T-I-M-E? Try taking an inventory of how you spend the 24 hours you have each day. Typically, many dads work for 8 hours a day and sleep for 8 hours a night. That leaves only 8 hours out of the 24 hours of each day. What do you do with those 8 hours? With whom do you spend most of that time?

I would not be surprised if many dads will honestly say they spend an hour or less per day with their families. By family time, I mean mental and emotional presence, not just physical presence. It's the kind of time where your wife feels a genuine connection with her husband. It's the time where your children feel loved, cared for, and valued by their father. How much of that kind of time do you spend in a day? It's sad to know that for some dads, they can't even be on the dinner table with their families every evening.

Yes, I'm fully aware of how busy you can be as a dad. You're working as hard as you can to provide a decent life for your family. You may even have side gigs or businesses outside of your full-time job just to make ends meet. I know how hard it can be. And because you always feel tired at the end of the day, it's a lot easier to just be passive with your family.

The fact remains, though. Being passive damages your family. Try having this hard conversation with your kids. Ask them what they want the most from you as a dad. Ask them if there's something missing. You'll be surprised – they will most likely say that, more than anything, they want your time and attention. They don't quite care how much money you bring home. They care more about your presence in their lives. What they want the most out of you is more time, more love, and more attention.

Being a passive father has serious consequences. You may not see them yet now, but you will clearly see them down the line, especially with your children. They always seek out your time and attention. If you don't give them that, they will look for attention from other people. Often, those will be their peers – people you barely know. You're not even sure if these peers influence your kids in a good way. More often than not, peers influence your kids in undesirable ways.

Not just that; passivity is damaging your wife too. How many times has she complained to you of not being there for her? For not spending nearly enough time with her? Has she also told you that she does not feel that you love, value, or treasure her?

That's not random. Those sentiments come from somewhere. Your wife is desperately calling out to you for time, attention, and care. Never neglect your wife – not only is she the mother of your children, but remember that she's the love of your life! You married her for that reason and more. You have got to show it. Make her feel that you indeed love her and treasure her.

When you shower her with love, you'll be surprised at the results. There will be less nagging, yelling, and criticizing. She'll become that sweeter, softer, gentler version of herself that you long for.

In the next chapter, you'll find out how important it is to treat your wife well. I'll give you a hint – this is the key to a happy, peaceful home!

Chapter 4: Don't Forget to Honor Your Wife

It's a common dad-related blunder to neglect your wife. After all, dads are always so busy working hard to earn a living for the family, they're always so tired once they get home, and all they want to do is rest and have some time for themselves.

Again, it's not a bad thing to work hard. The need for rest after a full day of work is also not bad, and so is wanting some time for yourself. It becomes a problem when you begin to forget about your wife in the process.

Remember, your wife came first before your children. You found her first, and you were the one who decided to put a ring on her finger. If you're like most dads, your wife was your choice. With that, she deserves all the love and care you're capable of giving.

Sadly, in most married couples, this is not evident. It's no wonder that many wives tend to complain about their husbands not giving them enough attention. For some, the husbands are away nearly all the time – too busy working to give their families a "good life." For others, the husbands are there, but really not there. In other words, they are physically present at home a lot of the time, but they are mentally checked out. Their minds are elsewhere instead of fully focused on their wives.

Attention. Affection. Affirmation.

The Scriptures actually give stern words against husbands who do not treat their wives well. The Apostle Peter writes, "Husbands, in the same way be considerate as you live with your wives, and treat them with respect as the weaker partner and as heirs with you of the gracious gift of life, so that nothing will hinder your prayers." (1 Peter 3:7).

Take a look at that passage again closely. Pay attention to the last part – "so that nothing will hinder your prayers." Shocking? That's probably why your life seems so miserable and none of your prayers seem to have been answered. Look at how you're treating your wife. Are you treating her right? Does she feel like a queen whenever she's with you? Or does she feel more like a maid or a slave? Or worse, ignored and neglected?

That's right, gentlemen. The way we treat our wives matters a lot to our Heavenly Father. He does not want to see our wives hurting because we neglect, abuse, or take advantage of them. Rather, He wants us to treat our wives the way they deserve to be treated – with respect, admiration, and unconditional love.

Now, ask yourself the question again. How are you treating your wife lately? Maybe you should ask her as well. Does she feel loved, treasured, and valued? Or will she tell you that you make her feel invisible? This aspect of our families is entirely up to us, fellow Dads. Never neglect your wife!

Attention

Our wives want – and crave – our attention. Try to remember back when you and your wife were still dating. Almost all of your time and attention were dedicated to her. You wanted to be with her all the time – from the moment you wake up in the morning until you lie in bed at night.

Then, you got married. And the time and attention just went poof. That's what your wife craves! That's why she's always nagging, complaining, and criticizing you. You think she's changed for the worse, but really, if you look at it, it's a desperate cry for help.

A principle in psychology is that *every behavior is a form of communication*. This includes what we perceive as misbehaviors. So if you find your wife constantly nagging and often in a bad mood, don't blame her. Instead, ask yourself why. Why could she be behaving that way? What could I have done to make her like that? More often than not, it's about something you've done or haven't done that forced her to behave badly.

So Dads, pay attention. Pay attention to your wife. Her behavior and actions are clues to what she's feeling deep inside.

A key aspect of attention is listening. Not just hearing, but *listening*. Hearing is merely the sound of her voice entering your ears. Listening is taking her words in and understanding what they mean – and reading between the lines if needed.

That kind of listening requires focused attention. You have to be fully present in the moment while your wife is talking to you. You can't be on your phone. You can't be watching football. You can't be spacing out either. Be in the moment and listen well.

Active Listening

One helpful technique is called *active listening.* This means you partici-pate while listening to your wife. You not only hear her words, but also tune into her thoughts and emotions.

To be an active listener involves three aspects: your brain, your emotions, and your behavior. The brain aspect is about cognitive functions – taking in the words your wife tells you and understanding them. The emotional part is about staying calm and composed throughout the conversation, no matter how your wife's words make you feel. Finally, the behavioral aspect is about showing that you're interested in your wife's stories through your body language.

A key part of active listening is echoing what your wife is saying across the conversation. I don't mean just parroting her words back at her; it also means asking relevant questions, clarifying parts you did not comprehend well enough, and checking with her if you're on the same page with what she said.

Active listening is one of the best gifts you can give your wife. It's not a material gift, but it doesn't cost any money. But your wife will definitely appreciate it. Active listening will make her feel that you truly value what she says. This is especially true because for your wife, her intimate relationship with you thrives on conversation. You listening intently to her makes her feel closer and more connected to you.

Practice this every time your wife talks to you, and you'll be surprised. She'll be more loving, gentle, and feminine in how she treats you. All because she feels that you value her words.

Listen without rehearsing replies

This is one thing many dads are guilty of, especially in conversations with their wives on difficult topics. It could be anything from money, their relationship as husband and wife, parenting, career choices, and big decisions to be made. I must admit, these conversations are indeed pretty hard to navigate. Hence they're called *difficult* conversations.

But that doesn't mean you should tune out. And if you keep trying to rehearse responses in your mind while your wife is talking, that's exactly one way of tuning out. It may be unintentional, but it's still taking attention away from your wife and into your own thought processes. Instead of actually listening to what your wife has to say, your mind is constantly manufacturing possible replies to her words. This is not active listening.

Doing this makes it a lot easier for you to miss important details and context. If your mind is always busy figuring out responses, you cannot focus on what your wife is really saying.

In the field of communication, it is a known fact that words only represent about 20% of the message. The remaining 80% is in what's known as *nonverbal communication*. This includes body language, facial expressions, tone of voice, eye movements, and many other things your wife expresses to you that aren't words.

Communication with your wife also involves reading between the lines. Her words always matter, but she also communicates things beyond her words. Those things matter as well. As a husband, you need to be sensitive to those nonverbal cues, too. You will understand your wife much better, and she will feel that you really do get her.

I know this skill may be hard to master. I myself haven't gotten the hang of it fully. But hear me out – this is really essential. Once your wife feels that you truly understand her, she will appreciate you even more.

Phone off

Again, let me emphasize one important thing. Active listening involves putting all of your attention on your wife. You can't say you're actively listening if you're also on your phone while talking to your wife. That's partial attention. You'll be selectively hearing things that way. You can't be focused on your wife's stories while dividing your attention every few seconds on whatever is on your screen. That's not active listening. Your attention must be fully on your wife at the moment.

If you try to have a conversation with your wife while glancing at your phone every now and then, it won't work well. This is not even genuine listening. Your divided attention communicates to your wife that she is not important, that she is not your priority. This kind of behavior tells her you would rather look at your phone than listen to her. In other words, it communicates rejection.

It's best to put your phone away while having a conversation with your wife. Put it in your pocket, or better yet, leave it out of sight. Put it in silent mode if you have to. You don't want any notifications to distract you while giving your time and attention to the most precious person in your life.

When the distractions are off, you become fully plugged into your wife's mind and heart. That's exactly what she wants. She wants that sense of connection from you. If you build that connection, you and your wife will have a much deeper, more intimate relationship with each other.

Affection

I'm sure you love your wife. If I asked you if you love your wife, you would most certainly say you do. The question now is: How do you show it?

Many wives would complain that they feel their husbands don't love them. Not because their husbands really don't love them, but because their husbands don't express much affection. These include the tangible actions you do that make your wife really feel that you love her.

For example, giving her hugs in the middle of the day, some kisses on the cheek or the forehead at times she least expects it, putting your arm around her shoulder while you're walking to the supermarket, and so on. Other times, she may want you to express affection with words. You could sing her a song, write her a letter, or if you're extra creative, whip up a poem just for her. If it's a letter or a poem, read it out loud, too, and make it extra special. These little things can mean the world to your wife. To you, it may be little, but to her, it's a huge deal!

Do things that show how much you love her and how much she means to you. This is one sure way to keep your wife happy each day. Expressing your affection also strengthens your bond and intimacy. Remember, if you really love your wife, you ought to be showing it. You can't just assume that your wife knows how much you love her. Well, she does know that, but she also wants you to show it to her as much as you can.

Expressing affection does not have to be overly theatrical like in the movies. You don't have to make grand gestures (especially if you cannot afford to). Even simple ones count. In whatever creative way you choose to express your affection, your wife will definitely notice and appreciate your efforts.

Affirmation

Your wife will also love it if you affirm her positive qualities. Did you notice something nice she did? Affirm it. Tell her about it. Tell her how she did a great job or how much you appreciate what she did for you. Does she show a particular attitude every day that makes you smile? Affirm it. Tell her how much that good attitude of hers makes your day. Does she dress in a way you really like? Tell her that. Affirm her choice of wardrobe. Most importantly, do you like the way she looks just as it is? Definitely do tell her that. Affirming your wife's beauty will make her eyes light up!

Affirmation is a powerful tool to build your wife up. Each time you affirm her, she feels better about herself, her confidence soars through the roof, and you make her feel like a queen. She may be having a bad day, but once she hears your affirming words, it's an instant pick-me-up for her. Actually, affirmation is not only great for your wife, but for your children as well (as you will see later in Chapter 7).

Your wife goes through a lot of negativity every day already. One of your roles as a husband is to alleviate the suffering from all the harsh words and treatment she may be getting from others. Affirmation is the best way to do that. Take the time and effort to affirm your wife every day. Similar to active listening, this is a great gift that costs no money at all, but something your wife will certainly appreciate.

Now, I hope you can see how important your relationship with your wife is. As a Dad, your mandate is not only to your children, but to your wife as well. You can't have been a Dad without her, after all. Value your wife, treasure her, and treat her right, and she will do the same to you. That's the Golden Rule at home.

In the next chapter, we'll talk about something that has some Dads at their wit's end – how to discipline your children.

Chapter 5: Disciplining Your Children

Disciplining kids is often associated with the dads. The stereotype is an angry father with a belt, a stick, or a paddle coming to whip his erring child. The purpose is often to get the child to behave properly. It gives the father a sense of being an authority figure, having the power to make his children do what he wants them to do. And it also makes most children fear their dads – make Dad mad, and he'll be coming to get you.

This sort of a Dad image might be effective in some ways to make kids behave, but it's not the best. In fact, all this stereotype does is paint fathers in a bad light: abusive fathers, dads who discipline in anger, dads who take revenge against their kids' misbehaviors. This is not what fatherhood ought to be.

The Holy Scriptures say in Proverbs 22:6: "Train up a child in the way he should go, so that when he is old he will not depart from it." This is what discipline is all about – it's training for your children. The discipline you do ought to train them to behave properly, to make good decisions, to be productive members of society, and to be good citizens of the United States of America.

Undisciplined children will fail later in life

Neglecting to discipline your children sets them up for failure in adult life. If you don't discipline them, how will they have a sense of right and wrong? What will guide them to make the right choices? How will they get used to doing the right things?

With a lack of discipline, your kids will likely grow up with disorder and chaos. They may cause problems in society when they grow up. They could end up doing drugs, going with the wrong crowd, or worse, getting involved in criminal activity. They cannot be good American citizens without your discipline.

Basically, undisciplined kids will do whatever they want, without regard to the consequences of their actions. They may not become criminals, but their actions may still be detrimental to them and the people around them.

The Apostle Paul mentioned this: "Everything is permissible, but not everything is beneficial." (1 Corinthians 6:12). That means your kids can actually do whatever they want. But not everything they do will benefit them and those around them. Some of their decisions can even be harmful.

Such is why discipline is necessary. It trains your kids in knowing what is good and choosing to do those good things. It also makes them aware of what is bad and gives them the skills to avoid those bad things. With these skills, they can better thrive in adult life.

Abuse is not discipline

Excessively hurting your children is not disciplining them. Instilling fear through constant displays of anger is also not discipline. Yelling, screaming, and verbally shaming your kids is likewise not discipline. All of these are called abuse. As a Dad, you absolutely do not want to end up as your child's abuser.

The wrong forms of "discipline" can have serious negative effects on your children. They can become traumatized early in childhood and end up with conditions like the following:

- Anxiety disorder
- Depression
- Obsessive-compulsive disorder (OCD)
- Oppositional defiant disorder (ODD)
- Complex post-traumatic stress disorder (C-PTSD)
- Attention deficit hyperactivity disorder (ADHD)

This is not even an exhaustive list of mental health issues that can arise because of abusive discipline. There are more, and your children may have to live with those conditions for the rest of their lives. In some kids, these conditions do not show up until adulthood. With that, they have to face adult life while managing these mental health conditions.

Of course, you do not want your kids to develop any of these when they grow older. No good Dad wants to be the reason for damaging his kid's mental health. For this reason, discipline must be done the proper way.

In the Holy Scriptures, it is written in Ephesians 6:4, "Fathers, do not provoke your children to anger by the way you treat them. Rather, bring them up with the discipline and instruction that comes from the Lord." Let's take a look at those two sentences more closely.

The first part clearly states whom the command is for. It's for us, the Dads. Then comes the clearcut command that says "do not provoke your children to anger by the way you treat them." This means your children can get mad at you if you treat them wrongly. They have the right to feel that way. The Heavenly Father will not strike your kids with lightning if they get angry at you for mistreating them! Likewise, there will be no fire raining down from heaven if your kids get upset at you.

Yes, your kids have the responsibility to respect you as their father. The Scriptures also say this: "Children, obey your parents in the Lord for this is right." (Ephesians 6:1). But the greater responsibility is on the fathers. We are the more mature persons, so it is our responsibility to keep our emotions in check. We ought to avoid making our children angry, especially when we discipline them.

Let me make one thing crystal clear: Discipline is not about making your kids suffer. It is not about inflicting maximum pain to bring about a sense of remorse. It is certainly not about shaming your kids into submission. All of these actions are abusive. They will damage your kids one way or another. The worst part is they will bring this damage until they become adults.

You must discipline the right way. But how can you do that? Let's go back to the passage in Ephesians 6:4, particularly the second part. It says, "Bring them up with the discipline and instruction that comes from the Lord."

This discipline and instruction is not harsh or abusive. Rather, it is firm yet gentle. It punishes wrongdoing but preserves dignity. It makes your child realize he did something bad without undermining his worth. Most importantly, it inspires your child to do the right thing next time – not because he's afraid you'll whoop his butt, but because he wants to do the right thing himself.

Such should be the aim of discipline – to correct misbehaviors. It should not strip away the child's sense of dignity, honor, and worth. Discipline should never be the reason for your child having low self-esteem. In fact, discipline should help him further develop his self-esteem.

Correcting wrong behavior through consequences

Different Dads may have varying opinions on spanking and other forms of discipline involving some physical pain (also known as corporal punishment). I'm not here to debate this, but I would say corporal punishment can be effective if used the right way. You may disagree with me, and that's okay.

In any case, I'm suggesting an alternative: *Allow your kids to face the consequences of their misdeeds.* This kind of discipline accurately mirrors real life in the outside world – if you break the law, for example, you will go to jail or pay a fine. Those are the consequences for committing crimes. In the same way, there must be consequences if your kids break your rules at home.

Suppose you have a rule that limits video gaming time to three hours each on Saturdays and Sundays. But your son decided to play Roblox for four hours on a Saturday. That's one hour over the limit. Instead of yelling at him or whooping him, apply a consequence. It could be something like, "You're grounded from the Xbox next week." Be firm in implementing this consequence. Don't allow your child to negotiate, especially since he already broke the rule. As he suffers the consequence, it will make him realize a valuable life lesson: "If I break the rules, something I don't like will happen to me. So I better follow the rules!"

Before you do this, here's an important rule of thumb. Always discuss the rules and consequences with your kids first. Clearly state each rule and the consequence for violating them. Make sure your kids understand and agree. Once they agree, you now have the upper hand.

Any time they break the rules, you can remind them that they agreed to the consequences. No excuses, no negotiations. Then, apply the consequences firmly but gently. No need to yell, scream, or threaten your kids with violence. Instead, be assertive and tell them, "We already talked about this. You broke the rules, and these are the consequences. Sorry, but you have to face them." End of discussion.

Here is another important part of applying consequences. While your kids are suffering the effects of their misdeeds, be sure to remind them that you love them. Tell them that you're allowing them to face these consequences for their own good. Remind them of the purpose of discipline, which is to help them become better persons. You're not punishing them because you just want to; instead, you're teaching them valuable life lessons.

Let's go back to our video gaming example. Because your child went an hour over the limit one Saturday, you decided to ground him from gaming the next weekend. On those days, intentionally talk to your child. Ask him what happened and why he's been grounded from the Xbox. Most likely, he will tell you that it's his fault because he played an hour too long last Saturday. Having this kind of a discussion allows your child to take ownership of his mistake. It teaches him to take responsibility for his actions. At this time, your child may have already learned his lesson.

You can take it a step further and design alternative things to do. Because you grounded your child from the Xbox, you can instead play kickball in your yard. Or you could play board games like Scrabble, Chess, or Clue if your child is into those. You can even do gardening with your kid, or have him help you wash the car. Any activity will do, as long as you get to spend the time with your kid. Along the way, tell him the value of this discipline you're imposing. Make him realize that it's important to make the right choices so he does not suffer negative consequences.

You never know, spending that time with your kid may have an unintended effect. He may enjoy the thing you were doing together that he'd rather do that again next weekend instead of playing Roblox. How do I know? Because I've heard it from a fellow Dad. Here's how his story goes.

This Dad, David, had a son, Josh, who loves computers. As such, Josh also loved to play video games like Counter-Strike. It's a shooter game that pits two teams against each other. The first team to either successfully detonate a bomb or defuse it wins the game.

This Dad made a rule at home for video gaming. Josh is allowed to play only on weekends for at most two hours. Otherwise, he would be grounded from the PC the next weekend.

One Saturday, one of the helpers in their house saw Josh play for six hours. That's four hours above the limit! When David came home, the helper immediately told him about Josh's gaming overtime. David confronted his son and asked him, "Josh, what is the consequence for violating this rule?" Josh, caught red-handed, had no choice but to say, "I'll be grounded from the PC next weekend, Dad." To which David responded, "There you go. No gaming for you next weekend. Sorry son, but you have to face this consequence. Even then, I still love you."

The next Saturday, Josh could not play Counter-Strike, so he tried to find other things to do. Turns out there were lots of other fun things to do at home. Josh saw what he was missing, and he loved every bit of it. That weekend, never once did he complain that he was grounded from the PC.

The next weekend, the PC ban was lifted, and Josh's friends invited him to play Counter-Strike again. But he didn't want to play, so he did something his friends may have considered ridiculous. Josh asked his dad to ground him from the PC again. That way, he would have a convenient excuse to tell his friends. David agreed, and he immediately grounded Josh from the PC again. The father and son then spent the weekend together doing lots of fun stuff that weren't video games.

This is one great example of how firmly applying consequences can change your children's minds for the better. Not to say that I'm against playing video games, though. Gaming is a good hobby, and I must admit it's a lot of fun. You as a Dad can even play together with your kids. I would say that's the best way to support your kids' hobby while guiding them along the way. Some games have violent and unethical themes, so it's good for you to be with your kids as they play through those parts.

My point is even suffering the consequences of misdeeds can end up as positive experiences for your kids. They will learn the important lesson plus a few other things along the way. That's how discipline should work.

Encouraging good behavior through incentives

Negative discipline (such as imposing consequences) is not the only way to train your kids. You can also use positive discipline, such as giving incentives for good behavior.

For example, you can reward your kids with extra screen time if they clean their rooms every weekend without you having to remind them. Or you can let them pick what to eat for dinner if they always empty the dishwasher after it runs. You can even reward your kids with new sets of clothes if they always put all their soiled clothes in the laundry basket consistently for a month.

There are lots more behaviors you can incentivize. Be creative with the rewards you give, and you can be as generous as your budget allows. Just don't keep on giving your kids expensive stuff; otherwise they may pick up a materialistic attitude. Splurging once in a while is a good thing, but don't overdo it.

Rewards don't even have to be grand or expensive. Even small, simple incentives work well to reinforce good behavior. For example, you can give your kids one scoop of ice cream every time they finish all the food on their plates.

The incentives don't even have to be material things. They can come in the form of added privileges, like this: If your kids finish all of their homework every Friday evening, let them sleep in for at most two hours more on Saturdays.

Positive discipline works because it makes your kids look forward to favorable outcomes. Doing the right thing then becomes an exciting thing. Another great thing about this is later on, you may not need to give them rewards. Your kids will make the right decisions and do the right things on their own, without expecting any rewards.

In the next chapter, I'll talk about a hot topic these days. It's one that many parents find utterly ridiculous. It's an issue that many parents have already spoken out against, especially since it concerns the identities of their children.

Help Another Dad Rise Up

Your Voice Can Be a Weapon for Good

> "Being a male is a matter of birth. Being a man is a matter of choice." – Edwin Louis Cole

Being a dad today is like stepping onto a battlefield. The fight isn't with guns or bombs—it's for your family's heart, mind, and future. That's why I wrote *RISE UP, DAD*.

There are other men out there—just like you—trying to figure out how to lead their family through this wild world. But many don't know where to begin.

You've already taken a step by reading this book. Now I'm asking you to take one more.

Leave a review.

It's simple. It's free. And it helps other fathers who are searching for truth, strength, and guidance. Most men buy books based on what others say. That means your words can help another dad start his mission.

Your review might be the reason...

- One more dad decides to fight for his kids
- One more husband steps up for his wife
- One more family finds peace in the storm
- One more generation grows up strong in faith

Want to make that kind of difference?

Just scan this QR code or visit the link below:

https://www.amazon.com/review/review-your-purchases/?asin= B0FKHP356N

Thanks for being a man of action.

Thanks for helping another dad rise up.

– Chad Allen

Chapter 6: Affirming Your Children's Gender

In this chapter, I'll be talking about a controversial topic, especially in this day and age. Other parents would disagree with me on this, but I believe that most will share my sentiments. I request that you hear me out on what I have to say.

In the past, when you heard the word "gender", you would think of only two things: male and female. It should be as simple as that, but today gender has gotten a lot more complicated. It isn't just male and female today; it's transgender, gender-fluid, queer, gay, lesbian, bisexual, and all the other things labeled as LGBTQ+. This world's idea of gender has gotten so complicated that they require an entire book to discuss the topic in full.

But that's not what we'll talk about here. What we'll talk about is the proper definition of gender and the role of Dads in this aspect of life. The Holy Scriptures define gender as male and female (Genesis 1:27). These are the only genders that God created. He, as Creator of the Universe and of Humankind, has the right to define what gender is. And in the Creator's perspective, a person's gender is either male or female.

It starts from conception

Even before your children were born, their gender has already been defined. Their unique genetic makeup predestines them to become either a boy or a girl; a man or a woman. Biologically speaking, you can tell from the makeup of the 23rd pair of chromosomes in human cells. If it's XX, a person is female, while if it's XY, a person is male. While there could be some genetic defects that blur the lines, those are exceptions and rare cases. Most people are still born either as fully male or fully female.

The Holy Scriptures tell us that the Creator made your inmost being, and that He knit you together in your mother's womb. (Psalm 139:13). This includes your gender, as well your children's. God has created their gender even while they're still in the womb. It may take a few months of pregnancy before you can know if you're having a boy or a girl, but their gender has already been defined.

Different roles

Both male and female have different roles to play in the family and in society. God the Creator designed man to be the primary workforce, as He commanded the first man Adam to work the land and take care of it (Genesis 2:15). Also, God ordained the man to be the leader of his household. He is to lead his wife and children to lead lives of integrity, honor, and righteousness.

Females have different, yet equally important, roles to play. The first female, Eve, was created to be a helper who is a suitable partner for the first man (Genesis 2:18). God did not want Adam to be alone, so He created Eve and told Adam to take her as her wife.

As a helper and suitable partner, God gave the woman unique abilities that only she could have. One of them is bearing children. Only women can biologically bear children, because their reproductive systems are specifically designed for that purpose. Men cannot do that, no matter how hard they try. No amount of replacement surgery can turn a biological man into a child-bearer.

Also, women are designed to be more in tune with their emotions. That makes them ideal as moral and emotional support for their husbands, especially in tough times. In these trials of life, it's usually the wives who help prop up the husbands from sadness and despair. It's the wives who help the husbands gain back the strength they've lost when they feel down. It's also the wives who often teach their husbands to also be in tune with their own emotions.

To clarify one important thing, I do not mean that women should not work. Nowhere in the Holy Scriptures is it stated that women are not allowed to work. The point is God designed men to be the primary workforce, not women. Thus, women can also work, but they are not meant to be the main breadwinners of their families. That's the man's job.

With that, we can say that God designed both the male and female genders with a purpose in mind. Each one has a different set of strengths, skills, and abilities that lets them fulfill their roles in the family and in society.

Preventing chaos

In the passage of Genesis 2:15, we also see that God charged the man to take care of the land. That means the man ought to prevent any form of chaos from ruining it. This principle also applies to the family.

For this reason, you need to affirm the natural order that your children were born with, including their natural genders. What society now deems the "gender assigned at birth" should actually be the permanent gender of children throughout their lives. This is God-assigned, and so should not be changed. Changing one's gender only leads to chaos in life.

The idea that a child can be any gender he or she wants to be is chaotic. I do not believe this will lead children to be who they are meant to be, nor will it cause them to live fulfilling lives. Gender confusion only causes trouble in children's lives, even into adulthood.

Back then, this condition called gender dysphoria was classified as a mental illness. Now, it no longer is. It s even celebrated every June, in what they call "pride month." People are proud of having confused gender identities. I don't think that's something to be proud of.

What sorts of chaos does gender confusion cause? It's mostly chaos in the mind. One day, you could be male, then the next day, if you feel like it, you can be female. Other times, you can even be both at the same time. You can be attracted to men, and you can also be attracted to women, or both at the same time. You could dress up like a man or dress up like a woman, depending on what you feel like.

See what I mean? There is no sense of order or logic here. Gender ultimately is based on feelings rather than facts. Your biological design no longer determines your gender. Instead, your subjective emotions do. With these "standards", there is no defining characteristic for gender. You can just be anything you want, whenever you want.

How, then, will the God-given roles of male and female be fulfilled if people are confused about their own genders?

This is a chaotic situation. As a Dad, you have the responsibility of preventing this from happening to your children. The way to do that is to be a guardian of their gender.

Start them young

Even as your child is still an infant, you can start affirming their gender. Words as simple as, "You will grow up to be a great man" mean a lot to the child if he's a son, or "You are a very beautiful woman" if she's a daughter. Your infant child may not yet understand these words, but these affirmations have great impacts on their development.

As your children grow, keep affirming who they are as a boy or a girl. If your son shows strength in his movements, affirm it through words like, "You're such a strong boy!" If your daughter shows care and concern in the way she relates with children her age, affirm it as well with words like, "What a sweet, gentle girl you are!" As you keep affirming these qualities in your children, they will better embrace their gender and their roles as either a male or a female.

As you affirm the masculine qualities of your son and the feminine qualities of your daughter, they will soon embrace the traits unique to their gender. They will have a strong sense of being male or being female, and they will bring this mindset as they grow up. When they become adults, they will have a strong sense of gender identity. Your son will know what it is to be a man, and so will your daughter as a woman.

In the next chapter, I will introduce a concept that will not only make strong, emotionally healthy children; it will make your entire family strong and emotionally healthy.

Chapter 7: Creating a Culture of Blessing

The family culture here in America is not exactly the best kind of culture to raise children. Sure, we have our freedom, we have a prosperous economy, and we are even called the land of opportunity. But none of that matters if our kids grow up in discouraging environments.

American families often operate in a culture that is shame-based. In other words, parents make use of shame tactics as the main way to enforce good behaviors. For example, a parent might reprimand a child in a loud voice in public for telling a lie. Public correction is a prime example of shame-based discipline – it puts the child into an awkward situation in full view of other people. The child is then forced to realize his error because of the disapproving looks of both his parent and the people around them. He would then immediately be convinced of his need to change his behavior. If he doesn't, he may face the same situation or something worse, like being cast out of his community.

Even if it's not done in public, shame-based parenting still has serious negative effects on a child. Imagine a parent blurting out a flood of harsh words to his child. No one else might have seen it, but the effects on the child can be equally damaging as public shaming. More so if the parent takes potshots on his child's sense of value as a person. Words like "you're so useless" and "you'll amount to nothing" will be forever etched into a child's mind when he hears them. Those words stay until adulthood, and they will have detrimental effects on his self-esteem and self-worth for the rest of his life.

Create a culture of blessing at home

Shame-based discipline is like cursing your child. Remember that the aim of discipline is to correct wrong behaviors without harming your child's sense of dignity. Shame-based approaches rob your child of his dignity whether or not the wrong behavior is addressed. The priorities of this kind of discipline are lopsided. It does not consider the child's need for the preservation of his value, worth, and esteem as a person. What's more, since every person is created in the image of the Heavenly Father, then all the more should a child's dignity be protected. God has assigned value and worth to your child, so you do not have the right to take those away from your child.

The antidote to cursing is blessing. So if you have been practicing any sort of shame-based approach to discipline, the time is now to change. You, as the Dad, have the power to reverse this harmful culture. You can be your children's superhero! All it takes is to create a culture of blessing at home.

This is easier said than done, though. Creating an entirely new culture to replace an old one is hard work. It takes willingness and intentional efforts from the head of the home. You have to model this to your family first. Show them how it's done, and show them you're serious in your desire to change the culture of your home.

The first key to the culture of blessing is protecting a person's dignity at all costs. That means when you discipline your kids, the focus must be on correcting their erroneous ways – that's all, nothing else. Avoid taking potshots at their character, personality, or anything that has to do with their inner persons. In other words, don't make it personal. Focus on the wrong behavior and what you need to do to make it right.

The best way to achieve this is by imposing consequences against wrong behaviors. Review Chapter 5 for more detailed examples. You can be creative in designing and imposing consequences; just remember to be consistent in applying them. Don't make room for your child to make excuses to escape the consequences. Also, make sure the consequences are appropriate to the misdeed. Finally, always remember the most important rule – preserve your child's dignity, value, and worth.

That last part is actually the most important thing in the culture of blessing. Make an effort to affirm your children's value as much as you can – even when you're not correcting a misdeed. In fact, in the culture of blessing, affirmations should far outnumber corrections. If you can affirm your children several times a day, then by all means. But if that's still too much for you, try doing it at least once a week. This is where you can build a new family habit.

The affirmation and blessing circle

An integral part of the culture of blessing is the so-called affirmation and blessing circle. I'll call it the ABC for short. You can start off by building this new family habit. It may feel awkward at first, but I can assure you the awkwardness will pass. It will only feel this way the first few times. When you get the hang of it, the culture of blessing will be your new normal at home.

Here is how to perform the ABC step by step:

1. Gather your family in a quiet, distraction-free part of your house. It could be the dining table or the living room (with the TV off).
2. Make everyone (yes, you too) put away their phones. You will need all the focus and attention you have for this activity.
3. Speak words of affirmation to each member of your family. Make them specific, according to the good things you see in them. Make sure to mention only positive words. There is no room for negativity in this activity. Do not criticize, nag, or even make suggestions on what each family member should be or how they should act.
4. Start with your wife, then the eldest child. Work your way down to your youngest child.
5. After you have said your affirmations to everyone in the family, make your wife do the same thing. Ask her to start with you, then the eldest child down to the youngest.
6. Make each of your children do the same thing. Follow the same pattern – the eldest child goes first, followed by the next eldest, down to the youngest. Each child may speak affirmation to their father first, then to their mother, and finally to their siblings in order of age.
7. After everyone has said their affirmations, speak words of blessing to each of your family members. Follow the same order as step 4. Make your blessings unique for each family member.

Let me emphasize the reminders in step 3. During the ABC, no one is allowed to talk badly about another. That means no complaints, no rants, and no lectures. It's called an *affirmation and blessing* circle for a reason. All of you already have enough experiences of being criticized, nagged, and told off every single week. It could even be every single day that you experience these things. The ABC aims to reverse all of these negative emotions. Everything that flows out of this activity has to be inspiring, uplifting, and encouraging.

If it's your first time to do the ABC in your family, awkwardness isn't the only thing you can expect. You can also expect tears from some members of your family. The affirmations they hear might strike a chord so strongly that it moves them to cry. That's okay, as crying can be therapeutic. Shedding tears is the body's way of releasing any pent up anger, frustration, and resentment that a person may have been hiding for so long. Once the crying is done, the feeling of release is so liberating that it can literally feel like a heavy rock was removed from the person's shoulders.

Fulfilling the longing for affirmation

Everyone longs for affirmation, especially within one's own family. The rejection a person can experience with his own family has huge negative effects. For instance, children whose parents routinely express rejection are more likely to suffer from low self-esteem, depression, and a host of mental health problems later in life.

Some children may turn to other people to fill their need for affirmation. They may find it in their peers, so they would grow closer to peers than their parents. Inevitably, they may grow apart from their parents even as they stay in their parents' homes. There would then come a time when they will no longer listen to their parents at all or recognize their authority. They would rather be with their friends than at home.

While some kids would turn to peers, others would enter romantic relationships early. Often, the attraction begins because their partners give them lots of affirmation and acceptance. Not to mention their partners also give them a good deal of time and attention. These things are exactly what they lack at home. As they crave the attention and appreciation from their partners, they will end up spending more and more time with their partners. The risk here is abusing sex early, with teen pregnancy as a typical result. Even those who use condoms, contraceptives, and other preventive measures are not immune to ill effects, which are mostly emotional and psychological. These kids may end up feeling used, objectified, and ultimately unloved by their partners. In turn, these feelings will fuel depression, excessive guilt, low self-esteem, and many other issues down the line. Some kids may also develop a distorted view of love and relationships. Young girls, in particular, may become hateful of men and vow not to enter committed relationships anymore with men. Early attempts at sex for girls may also be traumatic, which can similarly trigger the onset of mental health problems as any other form of childhood trauma.

Some kids may even turn to substances. Alcohol and different kinds of drugs can artificially trigger brain states similar to feelings of affirmation. Because these kids long for that feeling, they would continue to drink and take drugs. The more they take, the more tolerant their brains become to those effects. Soon enough, they will have to take more drugs or drink more alcohol to get the same effects as before. The cycle continues, in turn making them addicted to these substances.

All of these are serious issues, but they can all be countered by establishing a culture of blessing and affirmation in your home. Again, Dads as heads of the household are responsible for creating this culture and maintaining it. It is your duty to lead your family into a healthy, positive, affirming environment. You owe it to your wife and children to make them feel most loved and appreciated at home. This way, they will have no reason to turn to peers, illicit relationships, or drugs to fill their deepest longings. You, their Dad, will fill these longings instead.

Chapter 8: Healing Past Wounds

Fatherhood is a tough job in itself. I would say it's tougher than any career, and being a Dad isn't even a paid job. You just have to do it. No one else can replace you as a Dad. It's a job that's uniquely yours.

Doing the best job you could as a Dad requires a degree of stability. Not just the physical and financial aspects; it also includes your spiritual, emotional, and mental states. Most of this is influenced by how you yourself have been brought up.

This is where the tough part begins. I recognize that not every Dad grew up in a home that took care of their emotional, mental, and spiritual needs. Some of you may have grown up in a home that's far from ideal. Some may have had parents who were addicted to drugs or alcohol. Some may have been brought up in abusive environments. Some may have had parents who struggled with a mental health problem. And some may even have grown up without a father. With these kinds of childhood experiences, being a good Dad now is a huge challenge.

Other Dads have the privilege of growing up in complete families. Their parents never did drugs, never drank, and lived as good citizens and productive members of American society. They had stable careers, decent incomes, and peaceful lives at home. But even Dads who grew up in these healthier environments could still end up having some of their needs neglected. Perhaps their parents did not know how to fulfill their emotional, mental, and spiritual needs. Or they were physically present but mentally and emotionally absent. Probably some of these Dads had workaholic parents who had almost no time for them. And some just had neglectful parents who chose to ignore their kids' emotional, mental, and spiritual needs.

These so-called adverse childhood experiences (ACEs) can severely affect a father's ability to parent his children well. It also affects his relationship with his wife. Overall, Dads with ACEs will find it quite hard to be a good Dad.

Generational curses

Your experience with your own father is a huge influence on how you will father your own children. If you had a good childhood experience with your father, you can pass on the good stuff to your children. On the other hand, any negative experiences you've had, you may also inadvertently pass on to your kids. This includes any abuse, trauma, or neglect you have experienced in the past.

On a conscious level, you definitely do not want to pass on your past hurts to your kids. You want to be the better Dad, so you resolve to father your kids the right way. You tell yourself you will never do what your father did to you.

The irony is no matter how hard you try, you find yourself doing the things you said you would never do to your kids. Your subconscious has taken over, causing you to unintentionally unload past hurts onto your children. In turn, they bear your burden, leading to emotional and psychological damage.

The past hurts from your own upbringing. The traumatic events you've had to endure in your own childhood. The neglect and the times your needs were not even recognized. These and other similar things are what are known as *generational curses*. If not addressed promptly, you can inadvertently pass them onto your kids. None of these are good things to pass on.

The buck stops with you

There is a hard truth about past trauma, hurts, abuse, and neglect that you need to fully accept: Your trauma is not your fault, but the healing is your responsibility. Of course, you did not willingly subject yourself to traumatic events. Someone else did that to you, and they will be accountable to their Heavenly Father for doing such things. Justice will be served for you in due time.

The process of healing, though, is entirely on you. You have to make sure you take steps to avoid passing on the curse to your kids. Remember, the curse only becomes generational if you don't do anything to stop it. As a famous quotation goes, "The only thing necessary for evil to triumph is for good men to do nothing." Do you want the evil of generational curses to keep plaguing your family? I'm sure you don't. So do something about it.

If you don't do anything about it, these past hurts will resurface. You may not know it yet now, but there will be a point in your life that these traumas will be triggered, and you may become an entirely different person. Surely, your wife will notice it. Definitely, your kids will see those changes, too. Those changes in your behavior will affect your family, usually for the worse.

Even if it's unintentional, the effects can be serious. Think about it: If the traumas you have experienced in childhood have such profound effects on you at this point in time, imagine what it can do to your children. You may not quite see the effects when they're still little. They may grow up as normal kids. But in adulthood, once something happens that triggers those past wounds, untold damage could happen to them. They may have to live their adult lives struggling with mental health problems.

For these reasons, you must make an effort to heal your past wounds, hurts, and trauma. It won't be easy, and it won't be fast. Healing is usually a long, arduous journey. There are times that you may go back to old, destructive habits. There will be times when you just want to give up. You may even get tired of life itself.

Despite these setbacks, the key is to not give up. The journey is tough, but with the right support system, you can get through it. Find people who are willing to walk with you in your road to recovery – family, close friends, mentors, counselors, therapists. The journey would be less daunting if you have the right people with you.

You will become a much better father to your children and a much better husband to your wife as a result. You will not pass down those hurts and trauma from your childhood. Instead, you'll be able to create a healthy environment for your kids – the kind of home that will help them not just to live a decent life, but to thrive and excel.

The value of getting help

Recovering from past trauma and hurts is extremely challenging when you try to do it alone. I would even say it's impossible to recover by yourself. You need help on your road to recovery.

I mentioned that it's a good thing to have close friends and family by your side. That has value, but they may not be properly equipped to handle mental health issues. For this reason, it's wise to seek professional help.

Find a counselor, therapist, or psychologist who is trained in *trauma-informed therapy*. This way, they will know the best ways to deal with the trauma that you have experienced, whether in childhood or later in life. It's okay to consult these professionals; they are here to help you. Don't think that you're crazy by doing so. Instead, think of it like going to a doctor for a physical illness. Conditions of the mind are also valid health concerns. Seeking professional help for your past hurts is like going to a doctor to cure the pain inside your mind.

To emphasize, therapy is not a one-time thing. It will take time for you to recover. You may even experience times of relapse. But again, keep going despite these setbacks. Consistency is key for a successful recovery.

Think of people who got addicted to drugs. Rehab from addictive substances takes a lot of time. Trauma has similar effects on the brain as drugs, so it will also take time and effort to recover from those effects.

Take the time to go on therapy sessions. Allow yourself to discover what causes you to behave in ways that are concerning to your family. Then, work with your therapist in planning how to manage these behaviors. Take those small steps towards change. Pretty soon, your family will see the changes you are working on.

I'm a Single or Divorced Dad — How Can I Be a Good Dad?

Being a single or divorced dad is a challenging path, but it's also one of the most important roles you'll ever fulfill. While the structure of your family may have changed, your responsibility as a father remains unwavering. In fact, your role becomes even more critical as you navigate the unique challenges of single fatherhood, such as balancing time, addressing emotional wounds, and guiding your children through the complexities of life.

You are essential in protecting your children

Even in a single-parent home, your influence as a father is pivotal in your children's lives. Protection goes beyond physical safety—it encompasses emotional, spiritual, and moral guidance.

Divorce or separation often disrupts your children's sense of stability. They may feel torn between two homes, confused about their identity, or unsure of their place in the world. You, as their father, have the unique opportunity to provide emotional security. This is not about shielding them from all difficulties but about giving them a safe space to process their emotions and fears.

When your children come to you with their struggles, listen intently. Resist the urge to jump to solutions or criticisms. Instead, affirm their feelings and offer comfort. Proverbs 18:10 reminds us, "The name of the Lord is a strong tower; the righteous run to it and are safe." Be that strong tower for your children—someone they can trust and turn to when life feels overwhelming.

Children need clear moral direction, especially in a world filled with confusing and conflicting messages. As a single dad, you may feel the absence of a partner in this role, but your leadership remains vital. Teach your children timeless principles like honesty, kindness, and perseverance. Use the Bible as your guide, showing them how to live in alignment with God's Word.

For example, if your child faces a moral dilemma at school, such as whether to speak up against bullying, use the moment to teach them courage and empathy. Share scriptures like Micah 6:8: "To act justly and to love mercy and to walk humbly with your God." Your words and actions will help them develop a strong moral foundation.

Today's culture is rife with influences that can derail your children's growth—whether it's unhealthy peer pressure, harmful social media trends, or misleading ideologies. As a father, your presence acts as a shield against these negative forces. Monitor their online activities, know their friends, and stay informed about the challenges they face.

For example, if your child is influenced by harmful TikTok challenges or negative content, have an open conversation. Explain the potential consequences and offer healthier alternatives. Equip them with critical thinking skills so they can recognize and reject harmful behaviors on their own.

Ultimately, your greatest act of protection is leading your children toward a relationship with God. Teach them to pray, read scripture together, and share how your faith has helped you through challenges. Ephesians 6:4 says, "Fathers, do not provoke your children to anger, but bring them up in the discipline and instruction of the Lord." Be their spiritual guide, helping them build a foundation of faith that will sustain them for life.

Why Is It More Difficult to Raise My Children as a Single or Divorced Dad?

Raising children as a single or divorced dad brings unique challenges. Recognizing these difficulties helps you prepare for them and find ways to overcome them with grace and resilience.

One of the biggest challenges of single fatherhood is managing time. Without a partner to share the load, you may feel stretched thin between work, household responsibilities, and parenting. You might also have limited custody, which can make it hard to feel like you're present enough in your children's lives.

Instead of focusing on the time you don't have, maximize the time you do. When you're with your children, give them your undivided attention. Turn off your phone, step away from work, and fully engage with them. Whether it's helping with homework, cooking a meal together, or simply talking about their day, these moments strengthen your bond and show them they're a priority.

Providing for your children on a single income can be daunting, especially if you're paying child support or legal fees. Financial stress may tempt you to work overtime or take on additional jobs, but remember: your presence matters more than material possessions. Kids don't need the latest gadgets or extravagant vacations—they need a dad who's involved and emotionally available.

Set a budget that prioritizes your children's needs without overextending yourself. Teach your kids the value of contentment and resourcefulness. Share Philippians 4:12-13: "I have learned the secret of being content in any and every situation... I can do all this through him who gives me strength."

Co-parenting with an ex-spouse can be a significant source of tension. Disagreements over schedules, discipline, or values may create stress and conflict. However, your children benefit most when both parents can cooperate respectfully.

Communicate with your ex-wife in a way that prioritizes your children's well-being. Even if the relationship is strained, resist the urge to criticize her in front of your kids. Instead, model grace and humility. Your children will notice your effort to maintain peace, and it will teach them the importance of respect and compromise.

Divorce can leave emotional scars on both you and your children. Feelings of loss, anger, or guilt may linger, making it harder to parent effectively. It's crucial to address these emotions, both for yourself and your kids.

Consider seeking counseling or joining a support group for single dads. Healing takes time, but surrounding yourself with a strong community can help you navigate the journey. Remember, your ability to care for your children depends on your own emotional well-being.

Being an effective role model as a single dad

Even as a single dad, you have the power to influence your children's lives profoundly. Your actions, attitudes, and values shape the kind of people they will become.

Children learn more from what you do than what you say. If you want your kids to be honest, hardworking, and compassionate, demonstrate those qualities in your own life. For instance, if you expect them to admit their mistakes, be willing to admit your own. Apologize when you're wrong, and show them that humility is a strength, not a weakness.

How you treat others, including your ex-wife, sets an example for your children. Even if the relationship with your ex is strained, strive to interact with her respectfully. This teaches your kids how to handle conflict and maintain dignity in difficult situations.

If you're dating or have remarried, show your children what a healthy, loving relationship looks like. Let them see how mutual respect, communication, and kindness create a strong foundation.

Your spiritual life is a cornerstone of your influence. Let your children see you pray, attend church, and rely on God in both good and bad times. Share your faith journey with them, and encourage them to ask questions about their own beliefs.

Integrity is another vital trait. Keep your promises, honor your commitments, and live in alignment with your values. When your children see you practicing what you preach, they'll be more likely to follow your example.

What if my ex-wife does not want me to see the kids?

Few situations are more heartbreaking than being denied access to your children. If you're facing this challenge, here's how to navigate it with wisdom and persistence.

First, familiarize yourself with your legal rights. Custody agreements are enforceable, and the court system exists to protect the best interests of the child. If your ex-wife is violating the agreement, consult a family lawyer to explore your options.

Keep detailed records of your efforts to maintain contact with your children. This documentation can be invaluable in court proceedings.

Even if physical visits are restricted, find ways to stay connected. Write letters, send texts, or use video calls to show your children that you're thinking of them. Consistent communication reassures them of your love and commitment, even from a distance.

When faced with obstacles beyond your control, lean on your faith. Pray for wisdom, patience, and restoration in your relationship with your children. Trust that God is working behind the scenes, even when the path ahead seems uncertain.

Romans 8:28 reminds us, "And we know that in all things God works for the good of those who love him, who have been called according to his purpose." Keep this verse close to your heart as you navigate this difficult season.

Practical Steps for Success as a Single or Divorced Dad

Let's summarize some practical steps you can take to thrive in your role:

- **Be present:** Prioritize quality time with your children.
- **Communicate effectively:** Listen to their concerns and keep them informed.
- **Set boundaries:** Establish clear rules and expectations, and enforce them with love.
- **Encourage growth:** Support their interests and celebrate their

achievements.
- **Stay connected:** Even when apart, find ways to maintain a strong relationship.

Being a single or divorced dad is no easy task, but it's a role filled with immense potential. Your presence, love, and guidance can shape your children's future in powerful ways. Lean on your faith, seek support when needed, and trust that God has equipped you for this journey.

Your children need you—now more than ever. Whether you're with them every day or only part of the time, your influence matters. Embrace the challenge, and know that you are making a difference that will last a lifetime.

In the next chapter, we will explore the role of humility plays in helping shape successful fathers.

Chapter 9: The Attitude of Humility

Of all the character traits a man needs, this might be the toughest but the most important. It's called humility, and I believe this is the foundation of good character for any man, especially a Dad.

Humility means seeing your wife and children as more important than yourself. It means prioritizing their needs over your own. And it also means prioritizing what they want over what you want. It's an attitude of putting others first before yourself.

Humility doesn't necessarily mean devaluing or forgetting about yourself. Instead, it's about prioritizing your family's needs and wants. You can still have time to take care of your own needs; just avoid putting those first. When your family knows and feels that they are your priority, their respect for you as the head of the family will be through the roof.

The most humble example

The highest form of humility was expressed by Jesus Christ. The Holy Scriptures detail Christ's life and how he interacted with people from different walks of life. He is the shining example of humility, as described by the Apostle Paul in Philippians 2:5-8:

You must have the same attitude that Christ Jesus had. Though he was God, he did not think of equality with God as something to cling to. Instead, he gave up his divine privileges. He took the humble position of a slave and was born as a human being. When he appeared in human form, he humbled himself in obedience to God and died a criminal's death on a cross.

Jesus Christ had all the right to boast and think highly of Himself. He could have gloated to everyone He met. He could have gone all loud and proud about his equal footing with the Heavenly Father. He could have demanded everyone to bow down to Him. Yet He did none of those.

He served people considered as outcasts in their society. He talked to Roman soldiers, tax collectors, prostitutes, and other people who are hated by many. And He didn't just talk to them – He healed their diseases, forgave their sins, and gave them a chance to lead better lives. In other words, Jesus put others first before Himself.

His birth itself told of how humble He is. Jesus was not born in a palace or a mansion like the rich and powerful of His time. He was born in the lowest of lowly places – a manger. He was born in an animal's place to rest. Imagine what it must have been like in there. Yet Jesus did not complain.

He lived his childhood as a carpenter's son. No fancy clothes to show off to everyone. No chariots to quickly take Him to wherever He wants to go. No slaves to do everything for Him. I'm sure Jesus had to work, too, as a young person. But again, never once in the Holy Scriptures do we see Him complain.

With the records of His life in the Holy Scriptures, we can see that Jesus led a humble life. His only companions in his journeys were his disciples. No armed guards, escorts, or fanfare (though He did have many followers). Jesus would even go alone often to different places, meeting and serving various people along the way.

Towards the end of His life on Earth, Jesus was unjustly accused of being a criminal. The people clamored to have Him crucified, even if the authorities could not find fault in Him. Despite the injustice, Jesus stayed silent. He neither raised his fist nor his voice to protest. He chose to go through with the penalty of death.

Mind you, this is no ordinary death penalty. At that time, crucifixion was the most painful and the most shameful punishment. Imagine slowly dying an agonizing death nailed on a cross for everyone to see. People will see everything – from how the soldiers nail you to the cross up to the moment you breathe your last breath. All of your pain and suffering is out in the open for the world to see. You don't even get to wear a mask or good clothes – criminals were crucified almost naked. So it's not just the pain that's severe, but also the shame.

Yet this is exactly how Jesus died. He endured a criminal's death, as the Scriptures described. No other person on Earth can get more humble than that. What's more, Jesus does not actually deserve that death penalty. He had no criminal charges. Even then, Jesus went along with the verdict. He subjected Himself to death on a cross.

Humility is hard

Even for Jesus, exercising that kind of humility is hard work. Being a human person like us, part of Him did not want to go through that gruelling death. He even asked His Father if it's possible to not go through with it. He knew of the pain, the shame, and the extreme suffering He would experience.

But Jesus still went through with it because He wanted to fulfill His Father's will. Making that choice must have also been hard for Him. But because He remained humble, the outcome was exceedingly good – the salvation of humankind.

For us who are not God, humility is even harder. Our natural tendency is to elevate ourselves. We want to be at the top spot. We don't want to regard others as more important. We crave the power, prestige, and prosperity that comes with being in a high position.

And that's normal for humans. Just look at the ancient ones who tried to build the Tower of Babel. They wanted to build it to prove that they occupy the top spot instead of the Heavenly Father. But they failed, and the Heavenly Father dispersed them.

We can see a reflection of that story in our culture today. Many men compete for positions of power and influence in the corporate world. Colleagues in the office would even fight each other for a promotion. Most likely they would use words as weapons instead of swords or guns, but the point remains – they still fight each other.

In this kind of a fight, the humble never win. These cutthroat, dog-eat-dog competitions require you to always think of yourself and what will benefit you. That's the only way you'll get to the top. Humility is the opposite – the humble always put others first, so if they try to compete here, they will end up at the bottom.

I'm not saying that power, influence, and humility cannot go well together. They can, but it's hard to be truly humble if your priority is gaining power. That's how it is in the corporate world and in politics, and it's the same way at home.

As a Dad, it's true that you are the head of your household. But try to see what will happen if you act like the stereotypical boss who loves to order people around. You will end up treating your family as slaves instead of loving them. To keep your sense of power at home, chances are you will use fear to keep the members of your family in line. Consequently, your family may always feel threatened, harassed, or used.

Sooner or later, they will feel unsafe at home with you. In the worst case, they may end up leaving you. In fact, a great deal of divorce cases in the United States are because of power-tripping husbands. These men make their wives and children feel imprisoned and constantly scared in their own homes. With that, it's no wonder that many of them decide to leave.

To clear things up, I'm not condoning divorce. I firmly believe that the Heavenly Father never wills for any husband and wife pair to separate. But if a man lacks humility in exercising his leadership of the home, and he refuses to change his ways, divorce may be the ultimate consequence once his wife decides enough is enough.

But an ounce of humility can go a long way. More so if you let it grow and it turns into your greatest character trait.

Planting the seed of humility

No one is born humble. Also, no one can become humble overnight. Humility is something that you develop over time as you practice it constantly. You have to make the effort, and the desire to be humble should come from yourself.

When it comes to your family, the first step of building humility is knowing their needs. Listen to the things they tell you repeatedly. Perhaps your wife needs more quality time with you. Or your kids want to have more playtime with their Dad. Or your whole family wants a weekend getaway with you. Whatever it may be, listen for those needs.

Then, do your best to meet those needs one by one. Begin with your wife's needs – you married her first before you had your kids, so she gets the higher priority. Then, take care of your kids' needs one by one. You don't have to meet all of their needs simultaneously. You only have two hands, and you have limited strength. Find out which needs are the most important and most pressing, then meet those needs in order of urgency and importance.

Gradually, your family will recognize your efforts. When they see you prioritizing them, their respect for you will grow. Most importantly, as you continue exercising humility, the seed you planted will grow. Soon enough, humility will become part of who you are – not just as a Dad, but as a person overall.

Once you can see the results of exercising humility, don't back down. Keep being humble consistently – be even more humble if you can. As your efforts at humility grow, so will your family's response to the changes in your attitude. You'll notice your wife being less nagging. She may even act sweeter and more affectionate towards you. As for your kids, they'll want to be with you more. They won't sneer at you or roll their eyes as often as they did before. Once they see your efforts, they too will change.

Consistency is key

As I just mentioned, you need to make consistent efforts to be humble. You can't be humble today but arrogant tomorrow, then humble again the next day. It has to be a daily exercise of humility. Much like working out, your efforts need consistency; otherwise, the muscles of humility will not develop well. More than that, inconsistent workouts can make you gain weight. Instead of being fit, you become fat! The same principle applies when developing humility.

When I say consistency, I don't mean you have to make grand gestures every day to show your family how humble you are. In fact, doing that can backfire – it can turn into pride and arrogance instead. The better way to be consistently humble is through small, intentional efforts. For example, letting your wife get the first serving of dinner, followed by your kids. Only get your portion of food when everyone else has had theirs. It's a simple gesture, but it would mean a lot to your family if you do it every evening. Or, when dining out, letting your wife or kids decide where to eat. That way, you're communicating to them that their preferences matter to you. In a nutshell, that's what humility is – considering others as more important than yourself.

There is no hard and fast rule to developing humility. There isn't even a maximum. As you practice it, you just keep on growing in this aspect of your character. The results will show in how you treat your family, friends, colleagues, and other people in your community. And if you're truly humble, it will be them who will tell you. You don't have to tell others how humble you are; they will know, and they will say it. That's the mark of true humility.

Humility strengthens your relationship

For married couples, humility is a foundational character trait for both spouses. But I think it's a more powerful trait for husbands. Pride, arrogance, and dominance are often associated with men, and these kinds of attitudes are often damaging to marital relationships. But when a husband is humble, he lifts his family up and they all soar together like eagles.

A humble man brings strength to his family because he recognizes he isn't always good or right. He accepts his imperfections. He is open to correction and better ideas from his wife and children. He owns up to mistakes and wrong decisions. He takes full responsibility for everything he does. With these, he never hesitates to consult his family or ask help from them. The best part is he has no problem admitting when he's wrong – and he takes the lead in finding a solution to the problem.

Humility is especially effective if you want your wife to treat you better. If you are always willing to admit fault if you do something wrong, and if you're willing to apologize and make things right, then your wife will see you in a much better light. She will see you as a real man – willing to take responsibility, not offering up excuses for every mistake.

Not just that, but your children's respect for you will soar as well. A Dad driven by pride is never a good example to his children. You will pass on that misplaced pride to your kids, and they will grow up filled with pride as well. If you want your children to have good character, it has to start with you. And it has to start with humility.

A humble Dad is not afraid to admit to his kids whenever he's wrong. He will always openly and honestly tell his kids if he did something that upset them. Most importantly, he is willing to ask for forgiveness right away. He doesn't let the problem stay for long; he addresses the issue head on. He then does what he can to be on good terms again with his family.

Often, a Dad's pride can get in the way of repairing a relationship damaged by conflict. Whether it's with your wife or with your children, the core issue is the same. Whether it's your fault or not, pride always gets in the way of reconciling.

But if you are humble enough to admit your shortcomings, and you take responsibility for your actions, your family will be happy about your attitude. Fights will not blow out of proportion. Problems will get solved more quickly, and you can figure out better solutions that will benefit everyone in the family.

A proverb from the Holy Scriptures says this: "Pride goes before destruction, and haughtiness before a fall." (Proverbs 16:18). Pride can destroy your family, and it can lead to your downfall. As a Dad, remember that you are the head of your family. You get to decide what attitude you put forth at home. If it's pride, the proverb clearly lets you know what it will lead to.

But if it's humility that drives you, the end result is better relationships with your wife and children. Your family will have a much stronger bond together as you model humility to each one.

Soon enough, all of you will be humble towards each other. Everyone will look after each other's needs before their own. The only competition you will have at home is outgiving each other and out-loving each other. No one will feel abandoned, insecure, forgotten, or unloved.

Do not neglect yourself

As I mentioned earlier, humility is not about putting yourself down or forgetting about your own needs. If you do that, it's the fastest way to burnout. Once you get burnt out, you will not be able to function well as a Dad. That's not something you'd want to happen.

Instead, what you should avoid is elevating your needs over your family's needs. Prioritize them, and they might end up helping you meet your needs. With that, it's a win-win. Your family is happy because their needs are met, so they will be happy to lend their hands for your needs.

Neglecting yourself and your needs is actually a form of emotional abuse. It's abuse against yourself. If that happens, you won't be able to effectively meet your family's needs. As a result, everyone loses. You can't help them, and in turn, they won't be able to help you.

Remember: You cannot give what you do not have. So if you're spent, you will have nothing left to give to your family. As you consistently prioritize your family's needs, make time for yours as well. Communicate this to your wife and kids, too. They ought to know. In those times, say that you need time for yourself so you can take care of them better.

To make it more clear-cut to everyone in the family, discuss those blocks of "me time" regularly with your family. If you have a habit of planning your days ahead of time, include this in your planning sessions. This way, your wife and children are aware of your self-care time. They won't be upset that you need some time alone during a certain time on a certain day.

As a Dad, your responsibilities to your family are huge. Not to mention your responsibilities outside of your family – at work, in your church if you have one, and in the wider community. You are the provider, the defender, the mentor, and the leader. It takes a lot of physical and mental strength to fulfill these roles all at once. Every now and then, you have to recharge too. This way, you can keep yourself healthy and strong to face more challenges ahead of you.

The path to humility is a long one. I would even say it takes a lifetime to develop humility. Again, you can never be too humble. There will always be room for improvement. But as you practice this character consistently, the Heavenly Father will see your efforts and bless your family with more love and care. This way, as you take care of their needs, they will also see your needs and take good care of you too.

II

BONUS CHAPTERS

In this section, I decided to give you, the reader, 3 bonus chapters that I believe would be helpful. Whether you want to create a dad's movement in your community with your church, a single or divorced dad wanting the best for his children, or wanting to learn conflict resolution biblically, this section is for you.

Chapter 10: The Art of Conflict Resolution

Conflict resolution is an essential skill for any Dad. It's useful both in his relationship with his wife and with his children. Conflicts happen all the time in any human relationship, so it pays for every Dad to have the skill of resolving them.

Here are two key principles to keep in mind:

1. When handled well, conflicts can allow you and your family to grow stronger.
2. When mishandled or left unresolved, conflict can destroy good family relationships.

With that, it is in your best interest to make sure any conflict reaches a healthy resolution. This way, your bond with your wife and kids will grow stronger for every conflict you resolve. Each of you will end up wiser and more resilient, too.

Before we dive into conflict resolution strategies, it's best to know first why conflict exists and what causes it. Let's examine the origins of conflict.

Why does conflict exist?

Conflict exists because people are not the same. Each person has different skills, preferences, values, and personalities. No two people will completely agree on everything, and this will lead to conflicts in relationships. Every relationship – from friends to spouses – has at least some conflict. For families, conflicts are common between husband and wife as well as parents and children.

From a theological point of view, conflict originated in the beginning of mankind. When the first man, Adam, chose to violate the first command of the Heavenly Father, that was the first conflict. The Father's instructions were clear: "You may freely eat the fruit of every tree in the garden—except the tree of the knowledge of good and evil. If you eat its fruit, you are sure to die." (Genesis 2:16-17)

But we can see in the next chapter of the book of Genesis that Adam did not follow that rule. The man and his wife, Eve, ate the fruit from the forbidden tree. That was the first sin – the first conflict between the Heavenly Father and man.

That set the stage for all the conflicts between people until the present day. Reading further into Genesis, we can see the story of the first murder, when Cain killed his brother Abel. Then there was another conflict between people and the Heavenly Father, when humans tried to build the tower of Babel. Their goal was to create a tower that would reach the heavens – a bit like our modern-day skyscrapers – in an attempt to prove they were better than Him. These conflicts grew more and more serious that He decided to flood the Earth and destroy nearly all of mankind. He only spared one privileged family – Noah, his wife, and sons. Everyone else was wiped out in that great deluge.

Then came a reset for mankind. Noah's family repopulated the Earth, but humans remained sinful. The new humans still created conflicts among themselves. Nations waged war against each other. Tribes fought for land. Even family members competed for wealth, influence, and power.

As time went by, conflicts continued to erupt all around the world. There were both small conflicts within families and big conflicts involving nations. And as humankind progressed, so did the death toll of their conflicts.

In particular, the 1900s saw the worst conflicts in recorded human history. From 1914 to 1918, the First World War ravaged the globe, claiming nearly 22 million lives. That time, it was called the Great War because of its enormous scale. But it wasn't the greatest war ever – an even greater one would follow. From 1939 to 1945, the Second World War raged on, lasting two years longer than the first. This war took out an even larger proportion of humanity – about 56 million people died in this war. All in all, that's almost 78 million people who fell victim to the two World Wars.

All because a few powerful people could not resolve their conflicts in a healthy way. See what can happen as a result of unresolved conflict?

Now that you know why conflict exists, let's go back to the family. It's time to examine the causes of conflict.

Different preferences

One major source of conflict for most families is this. Each person – especially members of the family – have different preferences for things like food, entertainment, people, and many other things. You may like chocolate ice cream, but your wife may not. Your son may like sleeping in on Saturdays, but you may not. Your wife may like to watch chick flicks, but you may not.

This is not to say differences in preferences are bad by themselves. They are not; in fact, they are by design. The Heavenly Father created each person to have a unique set of preferences, and that's a good thing. Imagine if everyone in your family liked the same things – the same food, the same movies, the same places, or the same clothes. There wouldn't be any conflict, but that would also make for a boring life. Diversity is actually what gives life color and excitement.

If differences in preference are the main source of conflict, this is not too hard to resolve. For example, if your wife wants to watch a chick flick but you want to watch an action film, practice give and take. This movie night, let your wife choose what she wants, then watch the film together. For your next movie night, you'll get to decide what to watch then. This way, both of your needs get met – only at different times.

Here's a tip: as a Dad, you'd want to make sure you allow your wife and children to have their preferences met first before yours. This demonstrates humility, as you are putting them first over your own wants. Both your wife and your kids will respect and admire you a lot more for prioritizing them.

Different opinions

Another major source of conflict is differences in opinion on certain things. This can range from something as simple as time management to something as far-reaching as politics.

Similar to preferences, opinions are not bad in themselves (except if they are based on false information). For example, you may hold the opinion that homeschooling your children is the better choice than sending them to a traditional school. This is not a bad thing, as homeschooling does have its advantages. On the other hand, your wife may have the opposite opinion: It's better to send the kids to school. Again, this opinion also has its merits.

Here's another one. Say your teenage son wants to go out with his friends one Saturday night, but you implement a curfew of 9 PM. Your son wants to stay a little longer with his friends, so he asks if he can be out until 10. You're thinking of your son's safety, so you want him home earlier. But your son yearns for independence and spending time with his friends, so he wants to be home later. Again, both these opinions are valid and have value.

When differences in opinion have to be settled, the most important thing to do is to talk it over. Never discount the opinions of your wife and children. If you do, they will feel that you don't value what they think or feel about certain things. Make sure to give them the chance to explain, to air their side of the story. When you listen, chances are you'll find that their reasoning makes sense. You may even be inclined to change your mind. Alternatively, your spouse or child may change their mind as well. That's the power of talking things through.

Disagreements in moral values

With this kind of a conflict, there is only one side you should take – the side of what is good and right. You would not allow your child to steal, scam someone, or be dishonest. With that, when it comes to moral issues, a Dad ought to stand his ground and insist on doing what is right.

The ultimate guideline we have for this is the Holy Scriptures.

For example, we see in the Scriptures that it says, "In your anger, do not sin." (Ephesians 4:26). That means even if we are mad at someone, we should not do things that will harm that person or cause trouble for them. Let's say your son got bullied in school, so he came home one day crying. You ask him what happened, and he narrates how he was mistreated by the bully. He is clearly angry, and he says he wants to get back at the bully tomorrow to "show him who's boss."

Here we have a conflict, you as the father do not want your child to pick a fight. But your son wants to avenge himself, so he wants to give trouble to his bully. In a situation like this, the Heavenly Father mandates us to stand up for the right thing – and that is to avoid committing sins when you are angry.

For this reason, you cannot let your son do what he wants to do. Explain to him why it's not the right thing to do, and by doing such, there will be negative consequences. The bully's friends might gang up on your son and hurt him more. Or someone in school might falsely accuse him of starting a fight. The list goes on. As a Dad, it is your duty to stand up for what is right, as well as to teach your son to also do what is right.

Instead, you can offer better alternatives that will still allow your son to stand up for himself. You can offer to go with him to his teacher and discuss what happened. If that's not enough, offer to go with him to the principal's office. By doing this, you teach your son three things:

1. Bullying is not okay, and you should stand up for yourself when you get treated badly.
2. Repaying a bad deed with another bad deed is never good.

3. There are proper ways of standing up for yourself, like reporting offenders to the authorities.

I'm quite sure you will have other similar conflicts with your kids that involve moral issues. You may even have some of these conflicts with your wife as well. Again, the important thing is as a Dad, you are called to stand up for what is good and right.

Conflict resolution strategy #1: Give and take

Now that we've talked about three major sources of conflict, let's explore how to resolve them. Remember, any unresolved conflict will grow into bigger problems, but resolving conflicts can make your family stronger.

The first strategy is called give and take, and it often works for differences in preference. Let's say it's a Sunday afternoon and you're all hungry. You're craving for steak, but your wife and kids just want pizza. Then it's wise to give your wife and kids their preference – go to a pizza place and enjoy your lunch with your family. Their preferences are satisfied, they're full and happy, and you end up happy as well. The next time you eat out, they will be glad to let you pick a place.

Conflict resolution strategy #2: Yield

Yielding means to completely forget about your own preference or opinion and let the other person have theirs. You may not get what you want, but yielding shows that you value the relationship a lot more.

Here's an example. Say your wife had a really rough week at work, and she always went home stressed the entire work week. You notice that she's often grumpy and easily annoyed by almost anything (hey, it happens, and it's not your fault). The evening of Friday, she walks up to you and casually mentions she wants to go on a beach trip to drown out all her worries. But it's also Super Bowl weekend, and you've already planned way ahead to go to the game. You've even told your family about it, and they agreed long ago. But this time, it's different. Your wife is stressed and needs some time to recharge. There's the conflict – between what you want and what your wife wants. You can't have them both on the same day. One choice must be made.

In this situation, it would be wise to yield. Yes, the Super Bowl happens only once a year, but isn't spending time with your wife more valuable? The Super Bowl will happen again, but this moment may be a one-in-a-million chance for you to show your wife how much you care about her. Go on that beach trip with her and the kids. Enjoy the weekend with your family. It is well worth your time and effort. Your wife will appreciate you a lot for it, and it will show in her actions after the trip.

Let's face it. Yielding is never an easy thing to do. Especially if you have to give up something you really want. But as a Dad, this is one of our duties – loving our families sacrificially. This is a reflection of what our Heavenly Father has done for us. He made the ultimate sacrifice of giving up His only Son, letting Him die so our sins could be forgiven. That's the Heavenly Father's Love. If you want to love your family the same way, you need to be prepared to make sacrifices for your wife and kids.

It's wise to ask the Heavenly Father for help in this matter. Yielding is not easy, but with Him by your side, He will help you exercise that kind of love.

Conflict resolution strategy #3: Stand your ground

Standing your ground is actually not an ideal resolution strategy. At first glance, it sounds selfish – your opinion should win over everyone else's. But this is not without basis.

Sometimes, standing your ground is necessary to uphold what is good. For example, your teenage son has expressed interest in trying weed, but you know it is morally wrong to take substances that can corrupt the mind. With that, it is your say as a Dad that has to stand. You have to insist that taking drugs is wrong no matter what the circumstance. You have to stand your ground on this truth.

Though it may offend your child at first, you have to make sure that the moral principles you value are always implemented in your family. If you do not want bad influences to enter your children's lives, like drugs, then don't let it. Explain to your child how valuable it is to keep his mind sane and free from addictive substances.

Stand your ground, set the example, and your child will soon understand. Later in life, he will even thank you for insisting that he stay away from drugs.

To emphasize the rule of thumb: Moral issues always require you – as the head of the family – to stand your ground. Insist that your spouse and children stick to doing what is good and right. Keep them away from wrongdoing and evil, as the consequences of those things are dire.

Growing through conflict

I mentioned earlier that when handled well, conflict can help you grow as a family. Now, you might be wondering how it's possible to grow through these difficult confrontations and conversations. Here, one thing is for sure – growth is never easy, especially through conflict. But you will certainly learn a lot from every conflict you resolve.

The first thing you can learn is solving problems peacefully. The enemy in every conflict is the issue, not each other. As a Dad, you are meant to take the lead in helping your family figure out a peaceful solution to every conflict. Set the example on how conflicts should be handled. Use this principle from the Holy Scriptures to guide you: "Blessed are the peacemakers, for they shall be called sons of God." (Matthew 5:9). If you can solve problems and maintain peace in your family, then you are beginning to get the hang of good conflict resolution!

Another thing you can learn is unconditional love for your family. For sure, your spouse and your kids are capable of doing wrong things. They have the ability to offend you or annoy you. That's part of human nature. On the bright side, we also have the capacity to love, and you as a Dad have the charge to love your family unconditionally. No matter what they do, no matter how much they can hurt you, still choose to love them. And because you do love them, you will do what it takes to make sure every conflict is resolved well. If you are committed to this role, your family will love you back.

One more important thing you'll learn is how to value each other's opinions, points of view, and preferences. In cases of give and take, you can best express that you value your wife's and your children's points of view by letting them make their choices. It shows them that they are your priority, not yourself. Soon enough, they will return the favor and let you decide based on your preferences. Because you modeled give and take, your family will also practice give and take.

In the next chapter, we will talk about being a single or divorced dad and how you can positively impact your children during this difficult season in your life.

Chapter 11: I'm a Single or Divorced Dad — How Can I Be a Good Dad?

This chapter was added to chapter 8: Healing Past Wounds. I decided that adding this as a standalone chapter in the bonus section would be worth having, since this is affecting millions of dads.

I'm a Single or Divorced Dad — How Can I Be a Good Dad?

Being a single or divorced dad is a challenging path, but it's also one of the most important roles you'll ever fulfill. While the structure of your family may have changed, your responsibility as a father remains unwavering. In fact, your role becomes even more critical as you navigate the unique challenges of single fatherhood, such as balancing time, addressing emotional wounds, and guiding your children through the complexities of life.

You are essential in protecting your children

Even in a single-parent home, your influence as a father is pivotal in your children's lives. Protection goes beyond physical safety—it encompasses emotional, spiritual, and moral guidance.

Divorce or separation often disrupts your children's sense of stability.

They may feel torn between two homes, confused about their identity, or unsure of their place in the world. You, as their father, have the unique opportunity to provide emotional security. This is not about shielding them from all difficulties but about giving them a safe space to process their emotions and fears.

When your children come to you with their struggles, listen intently. Resist the urge to jump to solutions or criticisms. Instead, affirm their feelings and offer comfort. Proverbs 18:10 reminds us, "The name of the Lord is a strong tower; the righteous run to it and are safe." Be that strong tower for your children—someone they can trust and turn to when life feels overwhelming.

Children need clear moral direction, especially in a world filled with confusing and conflicting messages. As a single dad, you may feel the absence of a partner in this role, but your leadership remains vital. Teach your children timeless principles like honesty, kindness, and perseverance. Use the Bible as your guide, showing them how to live in alignment with God's Word.

For example, if your child faces a moral dilemma at school, such as whether to speak up against bullying, use the moment to teach them courage and empathy. Share scriptures like Micah 6:8: "To act justly and to love mercy and to walk humbly with your God." Your words and actions will help them develop a strong moral foundation.

Today's culture is rife with influences that can derail your children's growth—whether it's unhealthy peer pressure, harmful social media trends, or misleading ideologies. As a father, your presence acts as a shield against these negative forces. Monitor their online activities, know their friends, and stay informed about the challenges they face.

For example, if your child is influenced by harmful TikTok challenges or negative content, have an open conversation. Explain the potential consequences and offer healthier alternatives. Equip them with critical thinking skills so they can recognize and reject harmful behaviors on their own.

Ultimately, your greatest act of protection is leading your children toward a relationship with God. Teach them to pray, read scripture together, and share how your faith has helped you through challenges. Ephesians 6:4 says, "Fathers, do not provoke your children to anger, but bring them up in the discipline and instruction of the Lord." Be their spiritual guide, helping them build a foundation of faith that will sustain them for life.

Why Is It More Difficult to Raise My Children as a Single or Divorced Dad?

Raising children as a single or divorced dad brings unique challenges. Recognizing these difficulties helps you prepare for them and find ways to overcome them with grace and resilience.

One of the biggest challenges of single fatherhood is managing time. Without a partner to share the load, you may feel stretched thin between work, household responsibilities, and parenting. You might also have limited custody, which can make it hard to feel like you're present enough in your children's lives.

Instead of focusing on the time you don't have, maximize the time you do. When you're with your children, give them your undivided attention. Turn off your phone, step away from work, and fully engage with them. Whether it's helping with homework, cooking a meal together, or simply talking about their day, these moments strengthen your bond and show them they're a priority.

Providing for your children on a single income can be daunting, especially if you're paying child support or legal fees. Financial stress may tempt you to work overtime or take on additional jobs, but remember: your presence matters more than material possessions. Kids don't need the latest gadgets or extravagant vacations. They need a dad who's involved and emotionally available.

Set a budget that prioritizes your children's needs without overextending yourself. Teach your kids the value of contentment and resourcefulness. Share Philippians 4:12-13: "I have learned the secret of being content in any and every situation... I can do all this through him who gives me strength."

Co-parenting with an ex-spouse can be a significant source of tension. Disagreements over schedules, discipline, or values may create stress and conflict. However, your children benefit most when both parents can cooperate respectfully.

Communicate with your ex-wife in a way that prioritizes your children's well-being. Even if the relationship is strained, resist the urge to criticize her in front of your kids. Instead, model grace and humility. Your children will notice your effort to maintain peace, and it will teach them the importance of respect and compromise.

Divorce can leave emotional scars on both you and your children. Feelings of loss, anger, or guilt may linger, making it harder to parent effectively. It's crucial to address these emotions, both for yourself and your kids.

Consider seeking counseling or joining a support group for single dads. Healing takes time, but surrounding yourself with a strong community can help you navigate the journey. Remember, your ability to care for your children depends on your own emotional well-being.

Being an effective role model as a single dad

Even as a single dad, you have the power to influence your children's lives profoundly. Your actions, attitudes, and values shape the kind of people they will become.

Children learn more from what you do than what you say. If you want your kids to be honest, hardworking, and compassionate, demonstrate those qualities in your own life. For instance, if you expect them to admit their mistakes, be willing to admit your own. Apologize when you're wrong. Show them that humility is a strength, not a weakness.

How you treat others, including your ex-wife, sets an example for your children. Even if the relationship with your ex is strained, strive to interact with her respectfully. This teaches your kids how to handle conflict and maintain dignity in difficult situations.

If you're dating or have remarried, show your children what a healthy, loving relationship looks like. Let them see how mutual respect, communication, and kindness create a strong foundation.

Your spiritual life is a cornerstone of your influence. Let your children see you pray, attend church, and rely on God in both good and bad times. Share your faith journey with them, and encourage them to ask questions about their own beliefs.

Integrity is another vital trait. Keep your promises, honor your commitments, and live in alignment with your values. When your children see you practicing what you preach, they'll be more likely to follow your example.

What if my ex-wife does not want me to see the kids?

Few situations are more heartbreaking than being denied access to your children. If you're facing this challenge, here's how to navigate it with wisdom and persistence.

First, familiarize yourself with your legal rights. Custody agreements are enforceable, and the court system exists to protect the best interests of the child. If your ex-wife is violating the agreement, consult a family lawyer to explore your options.

Keep detailed records of your efforts to maintain contact with your children. This documentation can be invaluable in court proceedings.

Even if physical visits are restricted, find ways to stay connected. Write letters, send texts, or use video calls to show your children that you're thinking of them. Consistent communication reassures them of your love and commitment, even from a distance.

When faced with obstacles beyond your control, lean on your faith. Pray for wisdom, patience, and restoration in your relationship with your children. Trust that God is working behind the scenes, even when the path ahead seems uncertain.

Romans 8:28 reminds us, "And we know that in all things God works for the good of those who love him, who have been called according to his purpose." Keep this verse close to your heart as you navigate this difficult season.

Practical Steps for Success as a Single or Divorced Dad

Let's summarize some practical steps you can take to thrive in your role:

- **Be present:** Prioritize quality time with your children.
- **Communicate effectively:** Listen to their concerns and keep them informed.
- **Set boundaries:** Establish clear rules and expectations, and enforce them with love.
- **Encourage growth:** Support their interests and celebrate their achievements.
- **Stay connected:** Even when apart, find ways to maintain a strong relationship.

Being a single or divorced dad is no easy task, but it's a role filled with immense potential. Your presence, love, and guidance can shape your children's future in powerful ways. Lean on your faith, seek support when needed, and trust that God has equipped you for this journey.

Your children need you now more than ever. Whether you're with them every day or only part of the time, your influence matters. Embrace the challenge, and know that you are making a difference that will last a lifetime.

In the next chapter, we will explore the role of the church in helping shape successful fathers.

Chapter 12: The Church's Role in Making Successful Fathers

The church has always been a central pillar in shaping families and communities. It's not just a building where people gather for worship; it's a living, breathing organism with the power to influence, nurture, and guide its members through the complexities of life. For men, the church is a critical source of encouragement and wisdom, teaching them their roles as husbands, fathers, and leaders. For families in crisis, the church is a haven of healing. And for every believer, the church stands as a fortress in the spiritual battle that rages around us.

This chapter explores the profound role the church must play in building stronger families, teaching men their responsibilities, healing broken relationships, and equipping believers for the spiritual fight of their lives. It will also outline a practical plan of action for how the church can transform families for the good.

Why Men Need Guidance

Being a husband and father is no small task. Yet many men today find themselves stepping into these roles with little preparation. Society often diminishes the importance of fatherhood or ridicules the idea of traditional masculinity, leaving men confused about their responsibilities. As a result, some fathers are disengaged, some husbands are passive, and many families suffer.

The church, however, is uniquely positioned to fill this gap. The Bible provides a clear blueprint for how men are to lead their families. From Adam to Abraham, Moses to David, and ultimately Jesus Christ, scripture reveals what godly leadership looks like in the home. Men need this teaching to understand their God-ordained responsibilities and how to live them out effectively.

The Bible commands men to lead their families in love and integrity. Ephesians 5:25 says, "Husbands, love your wives, just as Christ loved the church and gave himself up for her." This verse emphasizes sacrificial love, the kind that prioritizes the needs and well-being of one's wife over personal desires.

Similarly, Colossians 3:21 instructs fathers, "Do not embitter your children, or they will become discouraged." This verse speaks to the importance of fatherly discipline that builds up rather than tears down. Fathers are called to correct their children with wisdom, not anger.

These are lofty standards, and they don't come naturally. That's why the church must actively teach men how to embody these roles. Sermons, Bible studies, and men's groups are excellent platforms for teaching godly leadership. Pastors and elders should take the time to mentor younger men, modeling what it looks like to be a loving husband and father.

Today's culture bombards men with messages that contradict biblical principles. From entertainment to social media, men are often encouraged to pursue selfish ambition, prioritize career over family, and avoid commitment. The church must counter these messages by reminding men that their greatest calling is within their own households. When men rise to their biblical roles, the entire family flourishes.

Helping Families Heal

In our fallen world, no family is immune to pain. Divorce, addiction, abuse, and strained relationships are all-too-common realities. Children grow up without fathers. Couples struggle to maintain their marriages. Parents find themselves at odds with their teens. These wounds run deep, and without intervention, they can lead to lifelong scars.

The church must step into this space as a place of healing. Jesus himself declared in Luke 4:18, "He has sent me to proclaim freedom for the prisoners and recovery of sight for the blind, to set the oppressed free." This mission applies not only to individuals but also to families. The church is called to bring healing to broken homes, offering the love of Christ to restore what has been lost.

Practical Ways to Help Families Heal

1. **Counseling Services**: Many families need guidance to navigate their challenges, and the church can provide biblical counseling to address marital issues, parent-child conflicts, and emotional trauma. Offering confidential, Christ-centered counseling can help families find peace and reconciliation.
2. **Support Groups**: Families going through crises, such as divorce or loss, benefit greatly from the support of others who have walked similar paths. The church can create groups for single parents,

widows, or those recovering from addiction to foster community and encouragement.

3. **Prayer and Intercession**: Healing begins with prayer. The church must actively pray for families in its congregation, interceding for marriages, children, and relationships under attack.

4. **Resources and Workshops**: Parenting seminars, marriage retreats, and financial planning workshops can equip families with the tools they need to thrive. These events not only provide practical skills but also create opportunities for families to grow closer to God and each other.

The spiritual battle

Ephesians 6:12 reminds us, "For our struggle is not against flesh and blood, but against the rulers, against the authorities, against the powers of this dark world and against the spiritual forces of evil in the heavenly realms." This spiritual battle affects every aspect of life, including the family.

The enemy knows that families are the cornerstone of society. When families crumble, communities fall apart. That's why the devil attacks families with division, temptation, and lies. The church must stand on the frontlines, equipping its members with the tools to fight back.

Equipping Believers for the Battle

1. **Teaching the Word**: The Bible is the ultimate weapon against the enemy's schemes. Hebrews 4:12 says, "For the word of God is alive and active. Sharper than any double-edged sword, it penetrates even to dividing soul and spirit, joints and marrow." The church must teach its members to wield this weapon effectively,

encouraging regular Bible study and memorization.

2. **Fostering Community**: Spiritual battles are not meant to be fought alone. The church must cultivate a sense of community, where believers can support and pray for one another. Small groups, prayer meetings, and accountability partners are vital in this fight.

3. **Encouraging Prayer**: Prayer is a powerful defense against the enemy's attacks. The church must model and teach fervent, consistent prayer, encouraging members to intercede for their families and communities.

4. **Addressing Cultural Lies**: The church must confront cultural narratives that contradict God's truth. Whether it's the redefinition of marriage, the erosion of gender roles, or the idolization of material success, the church must provide a biblical perspective to counter these lies.

A Plan of Action to Change the Family for Good

Transforming families requires intentionality. The church must take proactive steps to build stronger families, support those in crisis, and equip members for spiritual warfare. Here's a practical plan:

1. Strengthen marriages

The foundation of every family is the marriage. When husbands and wives are united, their children thrive. The church can strengthen marriages through:

- **Premarital Counseling**: Preparing couples for a lifetime commitment grounded in faith.
- **Marriage Enrichment Programs**: Hosting retreats, date nights, and

workshops to help couples reconnect and resolve conflicts.

- **Mentorship**: Pairing young couples with seasoned Christian couples who can provide guidance and encouragement.

2. Empower fathers

Strong fathers create strong families. The church can empower dads by:

- **Hosting Men's Groups**: Offering regular gatherings where fathers can share struggles, study scripture, and learn practical parenting skills.
- **Encouraging Accountability**: Creating small groups where men hold each other accountable in their roles as husbands and fathers.
- **Providing Resources**: Sharing books, podcasts, and sermon series on godly fatherhood.

3. Support single-parent families

Single-parent families often face unique challenges, but the church can step in to provide support by:

- **Creating Support Networks**: Connecting single parents with mentors and peers who can offer practical help and emotional encouragement.
- **Offering Childcare**: Providing childcare services during church events so single parents can participate fully.
- **Meeting Financial Needs**: Organizing benevolence funds or meal trains to assist single parents in times of need.

4. Equip families spiritually

The spiritual health of a family is paramount. The church can strengthen families' faith by:

- **Encouraging Family Worship**: Teaching families how to pray, read scripture, and worship together at home.
- **Hosting Family Events**: Creating opportunities for families to grow together, such as family game nights, service projects, or outdoor retreats.
- **Teaching Apologetics**: Equipping parents and children to defend their faith in a skeptical world.

5. Engage the community

The church's mission doesn't stop at its walls. To truly transform families, the church must engage with the broader community by:

- **Hosting Outreach Events**: Offering free parenting seminars, financial workshops, or counseling services to the public.
- **Partnering with Schools**: Collaborating with local schools to provide mentorship programs, tutoring, or after-school activities.
- **Advocating for Families**: Speaking out on issues that affect families, such as education, addiction recovery, and poverty.

The church's role in shaping families cannot be overstated. It has the power to teach men their God-given roles, bring healing to broken relationships, and equip its members for the spiritual battle of their lives. But this work requires intentionality, effort, and faith.

As a church, let us rise to the challenge. Let us pour into the lives of fathers, mothers, and children, showing them the love of Christ and equipping them with the tools they need to thrive. When the church takes its rightful place as a cornerstone of family life, the impact will ripple through generations, transforming not only individual homes but entire communities.

Let us take up the mantle and commit to this vital mission. The time to act is now.

In the next chapter, we'll wrap up everything we learned into a nice summary so that you can embrace your role as the spiritual leader of your family.

Chapter 13: Wrapping Everything Up

If you've reached this point of the book, then great job! You've almost reached the end. But it'll just be the end of the *book*; your journey as a Dad is far from done.

From the beginning, you may have noticed that being a Dad is indeed a tough job. I would say it's the toughest job in the world. You have lots of roles – mentor, soldier, rescuer, medic, manager, and more. None of these come with any hazard pay, overtime pay, or special monetary perks. Actually, being a Dad does not even come with a salary at all. Yet, you get to be a Dad 24 hours a day, 7 days a week, 365 days a year for as long as your children are living.

It's no surprise, then, that many Dads are not fulfilling their roles properly. It's tough, and a lot tougher in today's economy in the USA where one job is often not enough anymore. I see many hardworking Dads working two, three, or more jobs just to make sure their families live a decent life. I think this is a noble thing to do, but at the same time, it's sad for me to know that many of the other important roles of a Dad are being neglected.

But being a strong Dad is crucial in today's world, where lots of outside forces are destroying the bonds that tie families together. I've talked about this in Chapter 1. The dominant culture in America today is not family friendly. It teaches fathers to be neglectful and children to be disrespectful. It teaches that truth is relative, so whatever you feel is right must be right. That leads to a complete breakdown in values and morals. Anyone can define what is "right" these days, so there's that lack of an objective standard to define what is truly right. We, as well-meaning Dads, have to do something and push back against this breakdown of the truth.

Related to that point is the main idea behind Chapter 2. We as Dads are soldiers fighting for the well-being of our families. We have to protect them from the ill effects of postmodern culture, so we can instill the right values and character in our children. We must uphold what is right, guided by the principles commanded by our Heavenly Father and recorded in the Holy Scriptures. One part of the Scriptures even talks about putting on the "armor of God," which will protect us against the negative influences of our culture today. We can also teach our children to don this armor, so they too can be protected.

Soldiers need offensive weapons, too. As the saying goes, the best defense is a good offense. Of course, we are also provided with a powerful weapon to wield called the Sword of the Spirit. In essence, this is composed of the Truths we can find written in the Holy Scriptures. These are the truths we must uphold and live by. And these are truths we must pass on to our children. These truths will also be their weapons to fend off the falsehoods thrown at them day by day.

I know, I know. It's really tough being a Dad. I get how that feels. I myself have those days when I just want to throw my hands in the air. Each one of us is going through our own set of battles; it's too exhausting to have to go through another one. If at this point you feel exhausted and frustrated, know that you are not alone. It's okay to feel that way. That's how any well-meaning Dad would feel.

Perhaps a comforting fact is you won't be fighting your battles by yourself. Your Heavenly Father will always be by your side. He is ready to lend a helping hand at a moment's notice. All you have to do is ask. He is always willing to come alongside you, fight your battles with you, and even secure the victory for you. When you feel weak, your Heavenly Father is always strong enough to lift you up and fight for you.

Speaking of which, the theme we talked about in Chapter 3 is certainly something the Heavenly Father will definitely help you with. You, as a Dad, are the head of your family, including the spiritual aspect. It's like being the director of a movie, and your family is the cast. You get to guide your family about which way to go and what to do next. It's not an easy task, and you yourself need guidance from your Heavenly Father.

Being the spiritual head of your home is a mentoring job. Your role is to teach and model, by your example, good values and character to your children. Your wife is also a recipient of this mentoring, and she too can learn the kind of character that the Heavenly Father wants all of you to have. This role is crucial, especially to your children, as the kind of mentoring you give will define who they grow up to become. Train them to develop good character, and they will bring good character as they grow up. When they become adults themselves, they will be persons of good character. When that time comes, and you see your children growing up into godly, responsible, loving individuals, it can be the greatest feeling in the world for a Dad. At that point, you would know that you've found success in this crucial aspect of fatherhood.

Now, being a Dad is not just about loving your children and mentoring them. Sure, that's one big part of being a Dad, but let's not forget one more important aspect. That's being a husband. I've mentioned this in Chapter 4, and I'll say it again: You married your wife first before your children came into your life. You were a husband first before becoming a father. With that, you need to exercise this role well. The well-being of your family depends on it.

Remember how it was when you were still dating the woman who was to become your wife? Those were happy days, I would think. Always full of anticipation, excitement, fun, and joyful memories. That stage should not end after your wedding day. The giggles you give your wife when you were still dating should still exist when you're married. Actually, it's all the more important to keep dating your wife when you're already married. Keep the spark bright and the flame burning. Make the effort to keep your love alive. Make time for your wife, give her the attention she craves, and give her the love she deserves. If you consistently give her those, she will be her best self every time. She will reciprocate, even if you don't ask for it. Not just that, but she will also perform her best as a mother. Honor your wife, and she will surely honor you back.

Next up on the list of Dad roles is disciplining your children. I've mentioned in Chapter 5 that discipline is not just about punishment for doing wrong. That's the usual idea of most Dads about discipline. Some fathers even have the wrong idea about punishment, which can be dangerous. Unwise discipline can lead to abuse, which in turn can damage your children for life. Discipline should never be damaging, as I have discussed in Chapter 5.

What most Dads are also missing is the positive aspect of discipline, which is encouraging good behavior and character. I talked about imposing consequences for bad behavior, but after that, I also introduced the idea of giving out incentives for good behavior. With that, your children will have more motivation to do the right thing and behave the right ways because they'll be rewarded. Soon enough, they won't look for the rewards anymore. Doing the right thing will become second-nature to them.

I also mentioned that discipline is all about making your children disciples of you, just as Jesus Christ shaped the lives of his 12 disciples. This takes modeling and being a good example. You have to show your children what good character is like and how to exercise it. If they see you doing those things, they will follow suit. Your character will become theirs as well.

Another important aspect of raising children is affirming their gender, which I've talked about in Chapter 6. This is one of the biggest things that postmodern culture is trying to destroy – the idea that we are either male or female. Each person can only be one of those two; they can't be both, they can't switch between one and the other any time they like. Children are even being told to take puberty blocking drugs if they do not agree with their "assigned gender at birth." You can even see young people all over the United States celebrating having a confused sense of gender identity. They're even proud of it, calling this yearly event a "pride month."

As a Dad, you have to protect your children against this illness of society. Your Heavenly Father had a hand in designing your children, and part of this design is their gender. You have to be the one to affirm the male qualities of your sons and the female qualities of your daughters. Boys and girls are designed to be unique, and they have to embrace this uniqueness to grow up as proper men and women.

I also talked about creating a change of culture in your home in Chapter 7. This is called the Culture of Blessing, which runs counter to the typical shame-based approach of parenting. Unfortunately, this is something that we have become used to in the United States. Unknowingly, we are passing this on to our children as well. But you have the power to change that.

The Culture of Blessing emphasizes the power of your words as a Dad to influence the lives of your children. It makes a world of a difference when you speak words that are affirming and encouraging to your children. Do this consistently, and they will embody the words you speak to them. Your kids will grow up living out the qualities you want them to have.

Not just that, but your home will be a haven of peace and happiness as well. Once you establish a culture at home that emphasizes using words to empower, uplift, and inspire, everyone will follow suit. There will be less shaming, arguing, and badmouthing. Instead, each member of your family will speak more kindly and compassionately towards each other.

One more thing about this Culture of Blessing. I also said that doing this in your family may be really awkward at first. Again, that's totally fine, especially if you're not used to it. Sometimes, speaking words of blessing may even feel pretentious at first. Even then, keep doing it. The more you practice it, the more you'll get used to saying encouraging words towards each other. Soon enough, the awkwardness will disappear. Blessing and affirmation will become a lifestyle. Once this happens, you will have created an ideal culture at home.

The best part is your kids will bring it with them as well. They will grow up full of love and approval. They will feel safest, happiest, and most accepted at home. With that, they are less likely to look to peers for approval, affirmation, and acceptance. They will have friends, but they will not depend on their friends to feel loved. With that, your children are a lot less prone to peer pressure and the dangers associated with it. Also, they are less likely to get into relationships too early.

Not only that, but your kids will also grow up mentally and emotionally healthy. Blessing and affirmation boost your kids' self-esteem. They will value themselves better and have more correct views about themselves. Their sense of self-worth will be high, which will help them build confidence. Later in life, they will succeed in whatever careers they choose to pursue.

Another thing is your children will pass on this Culture of Blessing onto their future families. Once you set the example and are consistent with it, this culture will definitely ripple through generations. Your kids may even tell you in the future that this is the best thing you have ever taught them.

Then, in Chapter 8 I talked about how important it is to address hurts from the past. The key principle to remember is this: If you don't do something about those past wounds, you may end up passing them along to your children. That's the last thing you want to do. You want your kids to grow up emotionally and mentally healthy, so you need to take steps to make sure no trauma is passed on to them.

One important thing to note is you might not be aware that you have wounds from your own childhood. You may only realize them once you begin to show harmful behaviors that keep repeating. Often, it's your wife or your children who notice those strange behaviors first. If you don't address the past hurts, you will continue to behave in those ways. Then, these will begin to affect your family negatively.

But if you recognize the problem and go through a journey of healing, you will be better. You can correct old habits and replace them with new, healthy habits. You can also retrain your mind to transform destructive thought patterns into more positive ones. All of this is not easy, but it's worth the time and effort you put into your healing process. Most importantly, communicate with your Heavenly Father through your journey. He will help you, give you insights, and heal your mind and heart from your past hurts.

In Chapter 9 is about that essential character called humility. This is the foundation of good character for any Dad. It is all about prioritizing family over self – their needs over your own, considering them as more important than yourself. It's not about neglecting yourself; it's about putting your family first. To be truly humble is to be like Jesus Christ, the best example of humility we can see in the Holy Scriptures. Despite being the Son of God, Jesus did not act high and mighty. Instead, he stooped down to the level of the people he served. He actually cared about people enough to make their lives better.

The same principle should apply to you as a Dad. You should want to make your family's life better. That way, they can also meet your needs in return. Not only that, but your family will be peaceful, harmonious, and thriving.

In Chapter 10, it was all about resolving conflicts. This is an essential skill in fatherhood, and it's a life skill your children must learn from you. Any good Dad must model healthy conflict resolution to his family. It's not just about apologizing if you make a mistake; it's more about working together to find solutions to problems. Ultimately, every conflict should make your bond as a family stronger. When you know the art of conflict resolution, that kind of growth is entirely possible. Your wife and children will respect you even more for your ability to use conflict to deepen your bonds.

In Chapter 11, it was an encouragement for single and divorced dads to still fulfill their roles as fathers to their children. Truly, it is much harder if you're in this situation. But being a mentor and a good example to your children is still possible – especially with the help of your Heavenly Father. Also, know that He will not condemn you for being separated from your children's mother. If you know you need help, can't do it on your own, and are humble enough to admit these things and ask Him, your Heavenly Father will honor your requests.

Then, finally, in Chapter 12, you saw the role of the church in helping you become a better father. One of their crucial roles is walking with you in your journey of healing from past wounds. They should provide you with a safe and welcoming community, where you feel free to open up about your problems. They should facilitate your healing by guiding you to the truths about yourself in the Holy Scriptures. Slowly but surely, you should be able to see how your Heavenly Father looks at you.

Also, the church ought to empower you spiritually so you can better fulfill your fatherly role. Fatherhood has a spiritual component. You need to know how your Heavenly Father designed fatherhood, how He means you to play the role, and what He wants you to do in your family. The church should teach you these principles and guide you in your journey as a Dad.

Concluding words

This may be the end of the book, but this is not the end of the road in your journey of fatherhood. This is actually a new beginning. With the lessons you have learned, you are now equipped to be a better Dad – as well as a better husband.

These are the kinds of skills they never teach you in school. You will not find a school, college, or university that offers lessons in parenting, much less fatherhood, in the United States. Yet being a Dad is the most important job in the world – a job that only you can do for your family. It would be nice to at least know how it's done right – and that's what I hope to help you with in this book.

Now, it's up to you to apply all the lessons you have picked up. I don't claim to be a perfect Dad; I believe only the Heavenly Father is the perfect father. But at least I could share the lessons I myself have learned over the years on how a father truly should be. If you see your new Dad skills positively impacting your family, then it's already a huge thing. You, along with your fellow Dads who have read this book, will be on your way to making waves of change all throughout America's families.

Remember, you are not alone in this journey. Your Heavenly Father is with you. Ask Him to walk with you, and use His Word – the Holy Scriptures – as your guidebook. For sure, He wants you to be the best Dad you can be, raising your children in ways that are pleasing to Him.

Soldier on, and be the best Dad you can be!

Cheers,
   Chad

Keeping the Mission Alive

Now that you have what you need to lead your family with strength, faith, and purpose—it's time to help another dad rise up too.

By sharing your honest review of this book on Amazon, you're pointing other men to the same truth you've found. You're helping fathers who are ready to lead but don't know where to start.

Just like in battle, we don't leave our brothers behind.

So, if this book gave you clarity, encouragement, or a challenge—pass it on. Your review could be the push another man needs to step into his God-given role as a spiritual leader.

Thank you for standing with me. Biblical fatherhood stays alive when we live it out—and when we help others do the same.

»> **Click here to leave your review on Amazon.**

Let's keep the mission going—together.

– **Chad Allen**

About the Author

Chad Allen is a passionate advocate for fatherhood, dedicated to empowering dads to excel in their roles. Based in Virginia, he is the author of *The Dad Creed* and *A First Time Dad's Guide to Successful Parenting*, where he shares practical wisdom and heartfelt insights to guide fathers through the joys and challenges of raising children. His work, praised for its authenticity and relatable advice, has inspired dads worldwide to foster stronger connections with their kids. When not writing or working, Chad cherishes time with his four children—three daughters and one son—and enjoys family adventures in the vibrant Virginia community he calls home.

You can connect with me on:

🌐 https://thedadcreed.com

🅵 https://www.facebook.com/groups/316737610648654

Also by Chad Allen

Enjoyed Rise Up, Dad? If so, you will also enjoy these books by Chad Allen.

The Dad Creed: Understanding the Role of Fatherhood for a Meaningful Impact
A small but impactful book that brings a biblical perspective on fatherhood. The book gives practical advice that works and finishes with creating a Dad Creed. This book makes a great companion to this book.

A First Time Dad's Guide To Successful Parenting
This is my second book, it is filled with solid advice and tips to help raise your children from a Christian's point of view. Another great companion to this book.